Quiet Past and Stormy Present?

War Powers in American History

HAROLD M. HYMAN

With a Foreword by Herman Belz, Series Editor

BICENTENNIAL ESSAYS ON THE CONSTITUTION
AMERICAN HISTORICAL ASSOCIATION
400 A Street, SE, Washington, D.C. 20003

A Contribution to Project '87

HAROLD M. HYMAN is William P. Hobby Professor of History at Rice University. He has held this position since 1968 and taught previously at the University of Illinois, Champaign-Urbana, and at UCLA. He has been a visiting professor at the Universities of Chicago and Washington, with visiting lectureships at universities in the United Kingdom, Mexico, and Japan, where he held a Senior Fulbright Professorship in American history and law. In 1982-83 he was Meyer Visiting Distinguished Professor of Legal History at New York University Law School. His work in American legal and constitutional history has enjoyed support from the National Endowment for the Humanities and the Ford Foundation's Fund for the Republic. His major publications include *Equal Justice Under Law: Constitutional Development, 1835-1875* (New York, 1982), coauthored with William Wiecek; *A More Perfect Union: The Impact of the Civil War and Reconstruction on the Constitution* (New York, 1973); and *Stanton: The Life and Times of Lincoln's Secretary of War* (New York, 1962), coauthored with Benjamin P. Thomas.

AHA Staff Editor: MAUREEN VINCENT-MORGAN

ISBN: 0-87229-035-2

Library of Congress catalog card number: 85-73602

Printed in the United States of America

CONTENTS

PREFACE

This volume is one of several intended to mark the Constitution's bicentennial. The complexity of the subject, combined with the requirement of brevity, necessitated the exclusion or slighting of many topics, events, and scholars' theses, and the minimization of all.

William Wiecek, David Brady, Herman Belz (the general editor of this series), and Maureen Vincent-Morgan (the American Historical Association's editor for this bicentennial effort) read this in typescript and none-too-gently urged me to proper channels, and they have my thanks. Claudine Ferrell, Thomas Mackey, Kenneth DeVille, and James Peterson helped in many ways. Librarians at Rice University, especially Ferne B. Hyman, and at New York University's Law Library and Bobst Library, where I enjoyed a fruitful academic year as NYU Law School's Meyer Visiting Distinguished Professor in Legal History, aided in locating relevant materials. The NYU Law School's Colloquium in Legal History, cochaired by Professors John Reid and William Nelson, was a splendid environment for research and reflection. I thank them and NYU Law Dean Norman Redlich for their hospitality. Rice University, in addition to other supports, granted me leave for that academic year, freeing time and energy that allowed progress on several research fronts including this one.

Sylvia Ross typed and retyped drafts, improving them as she went. All errors are, of course, my own.

The reality of the history of war and emergency powers under the 1787 Constitution is that no single approach satisfied. I found myself inquiring, depending on the incident, into aspects of the history of separation-of-powers, executive power, judicial review, emergency power, federal policies in nonwar, near-war, and declared war situations, and uses of state militias and sometimes federal troops as strikebreaking police, among other topics.

My decision was to recount major events in roughly chronological order, and as much as possible to avoid committing myself to adversary sides in policy arguments, a decision that accepts the advice offered almost a century ago by Columbia University historian William A. Dunning in a letter to Frederick Bancroft: "This [adversary posture] is all right for a lawyer making out a case, but doesn't strike me as the most desirable method [for historians] to adopt."[1]

FOREWORD

Bicentennial Essays on the Constitution are published by the American Historical Association as part of its commemoration of the two hundredth anniversary of the framing and adoption of the United States Constitution. The essays are intended to provide students and teachers of American history with concise interpretive accounts of the most important aspects of American constitutional development. These essays epitomize the best recent scholarship in a field that, despite changing intellectual fashions, continues to make significant contributions to understanding our national past.

Because the United States Constitution is, at the very least, a written instrument of government that declares itself to be the supreme law of the land, constitutional change in America has been more legalistic in nature and juridical in technique than in most modern states. Either explicitly or inferentially, constitutional morality in the United States has always insisted on fidelity to the Framers' text as the touchstone of governmental legitimacy. This fact has enabled the courts to play a conspicuous role in the settlement of constitutional controversies. Nevertheless, in our study of history we recognize the political as well as the legalistic dimension of the constitutional polity. Constitutions are intended to achieve basic political purposes and hence juxtapose considerations of legal right and political expediency. Inherent in the concept of constitutionalism is a tension between law and politics, and this tension is reflected in our approach to American constitutional history.

Edward S. Corwin, perhaps the greatest American constitutional historian, illustrated the law versus politics dichotomy in a long forgotten, yet revealing analysis of constitutional change written in the momentous early days of the New Deal. Attempting to evaluate the impact of the astonishingly broad National Industrial Recovery Act, the centerpiece of New Deal constitutionalism, Corwin suggested that the very character of the Constitution was changing. He wrote that the Constitution was becoming more political and less legalistic. No longer merely a lawyer's document cataloguing restraints on government, it was being transformed into a constructive instrument of social purpose. Corwin predicted that in the future the constitutional text would be less important in the conduct of government and politics: like the Magna Carta in English history, the Constitution would be absorbed into a complex environment of political and administrative institutions.

Corwin was wrong, of course, in predicting the desuetude of the written Constitution and the decline of legalism in American government. His brand of liberalism was oriented to legislative policymaking, and he could scarcely anticipate the liberalism of more recent decades, which calls on judicial-activist judges to fashion public policy and advance political ends by interpreting open-textured constitutional provisions. Nevertheless, Corwin's analysis identifies the essential elements in our constitutional tradition and offers guidance for the study of constitutional history.

As the Constitution is more than a documentary text, so constitutional history comprises much more than a record of the development of constitutional law under judicial auspices. The Constitution is the complex of principles, institutions, laws, practices, and internalized attitudes and beliefs by which the American people organize and carry on their political and governmental life. Concerned for the most part with procedural matters, the Constitution is nevertheless ultimately distinguished by the substantive political values it embodies and promotes. The purpose of the Constitution is twofold. It creates government power for the promotion of the public welfare and the maintenance of public order and security. The Constitution also defines and limits that power in order to preserve individual liberty and social freedom. In the twentieth century the purposes as well as the techniques of constitutional government have been broadened to include forms of social justice and security undreamt of by the Founders. Yet individual rights and immunity against government power remain the bedrock values of American constitutionalism.

The organizing principles of the American Constitution have also remained remarkably stable across two centuries of political experience. These principles are the idea of self-government and majority rule; separation of powers; federalism; and the priority of the written Constitution as the source and symbol of governmental legitimacy. Within the institutional structures that embody these fundamental ideas, the principal actors in the American constitutional system pursue the ends and purposes of the polity. Lawmakers, executives, judges, and administrative agencies in the federal government and the states are responsible for making public policy. Political parties, interest groups, and the media organize, shape, and communicate public opinion as intermediate institutions between government officials and the electorate. Finally, the people as constituent power and ultimate sovereign give general direction to policymakers and hold public officials accountable.

Part of the appeal of constitutional history lies in its ability to illuminate the social, political, economic, cultural, and religious conflicts that give rise to and are expressed in constitutional controversies. Yet to understand the process of historical change, it is not enough to identify the values, purposes, and aspirations of conflicting political and social interests. It is also necessary to observe the way in which the constitutional system shapes the substantive social conflicts that are presented to it for resolution. The

Constitution sets limits on what can be done by limiting government power and guaranteeing individual rights. It prescribes the basic procedures for policymaking and designates the forums within which policy conflicts are to be resolved. American constitutionalism thus establishes the institutional framework and ordains the specific methods by which the American people conduct their political and governmental existence. The origin and development of this distinctive form of constitutionalism provide the subject matter of *Bicentennial Essays on the Constitution.*

Herman Belz, Series Editor
Professor of History
University of Maryland

To Joshua, the first

Quiet Past and Stormy Present?

War Powers in American History

HAROLD M. HYMAN

"The dogmas of the quiet past are inadequate to the stormy present," President Abraham Lincoln advised Americans in his State of the Union message to Congress in December 1862. A year later, Lincoln reminded Americans that they "must not lose sight of the fact that the war power is still our main reliance."[1]

These two statements are a useful shorthand for the American attitude toward the war and emergency powers outlined in the Constitution. Sometimes, in contexts of despair such as the one that evoked Lincoln's sad comment of 1862, sheer discouragement has eroded faith in the relevance of a constitution to the "stormy present" and of a constitutional history and structure based on perceptions of the "quiet past" of 1787. At other times, as in 1863, the relationship between history and the Constitution has become both better understood and more meaningful. Lincoln advised Americans never to forget that the war powers, "our main reliance," were (and are) part of the living (that is, evolving, relevant, adequate, useful) Constitution of 1787.

Americans have frequently forgotten this. Often in the most heated possible political contexts, therefore, they have to be reminded that the nature and limits of war and emergency powers under the Constitution are not precisely clear and need to be examined. Perhaps that is as it should be; perhaps the burdens and benefits of the 1787 Constitution, with its complex and often cumbersome procedures, and mixtures of specifics and ambiguities, can be better borne, especially in crisis, by creating the Constitution afresh, as it were, in appropriate ways.

Like people in most societies, Americans have had to grapple with foreign wars and domestic emergencies. Unlike other peoples, Americans began and continue their national life with governing arrangements and attitudes about government—some valid and enduring, others invalid and temporary—that shape their responses to wars and crises. The valid and enduring arrangements include political democracy, calendared elections even during wars, checks and balances and separation of powers between the branches of government and the two houses of Congress, and judicial review. The most valid and enduring attitude is constitutionalism, in which government requires constraints, as in a written constitution, but simultaneously must fulfill the demands that war or other emergencies place on it. This attitude, expressed through the politics of democracy, affects the formal constitutional arrangements, procedures, and institutions that permit changes and encourage diversity of views. From the nation's infancy, contenders for alternative public policies, including wars, have almost always accepted the 1787 Constitution as the principal definer of the limits of actions. Acceptance of the Constitution has not, however, meant agreement about it. Instead, almost every war-crisis clause in the Constitution has generated lively disagreement among the president, Congress, and the Supreme Court, and between the central government and the states.

Scholars and jurists have nevertheless insisted that the intentions of the Framers should govern war-emergency policies, but despite diligent digs into the available printed and manuscript records, these intentions have remained disputed and unclear. The seemingly fixed procedures of the 1787 Constitution generate varying constitutional positions about the war powers. In our own day, for example, public opinion is in flux about the civilian and military implications of atomic weaponry. Advocates of conflicting public policies on nuclear weapons contest each other in elections, legislation, treaties, and constitutional litigations, all in the context of the 1787 Constitution, thus re-raising the substance of Lincoln's fear of 1862: that arrangements and attitudes in an eighteenth-century document form a basically irrelevant "dogma of the quiet past" that is "inadequate to the stormy present." Because Americans often share this fear, it is appropriate to heed the poet W. H. Auden, who wrote that history is the "madonna of silences/to whom we turn/When we have lost control."[2]

A look into the not-so-quiet past is in order to learn if Americans have in their "stormy present" lost control of that center of many storms, the war powers, and to learn if the insight of T. S. Eliot's last *Quartet* is relevant: "The end of our exploring will be to arrive where we started and see the place for the first time."[3]

I

Defining War Powers, 1783-1815

The Framers of the Constitution spent much time and thought on the novel office of the president, especially the commander-in-chief's duties with the federal army and navy and the state militias, but neither the Framers nor the ratifiers of the Constitution specified much about war or crisis powers. This suggests that large areas of agreement existed. Among widely shared assumptions were Enlightenment precepts, which encouraged nations to fight only "just" wars and to restrain the conduct of troops, at least in international combat. Major theorists frequently read in America during the eighteenth century, such as John Locke, Charles de Montesquieu, and Emmerich de Vattel, accepted war and coercion as parts of life; so, necessarily, did America's revolutionary generation.

Constitutional Bases for War Powers

In order to achieve independence, Americans developed techniques to manage war in their newly created states. The Continental and Confederation congresses forged adequate links both to constituent states and to supportive foreign monarchies, while suppressing Tories and resisting the British army. Survival in a predatory world required a national military capacity.

Social and economic instability plagued several of the American states, some of which, like foreign powers, ignored the treaty obligations of the infant union. Eastward, the long Atlantic flanks of the thirteen states were exposed to seaborne depredations and even invasions. Visions of new frontiers to the North, South, and especially West invited retaliation from resentful Indians and European colonial powers, particularly revengeful Britain. Southerners worried about the adequacy of their local military forces to deal with always feared slave uprisings. Many individuals, while yearning for keener martial instruments of national unity and governmental effectiveness, also feared military dictators, a fear that President George Washington helped to lessen with his 1783 appeal to restless army officers to obey civilian overlords. This fear would endure as a commitment to civilian domination in civil-military relationships.

Leaders in the Revolution had, as in the Declaration of Independence, denounced the English monarchs who unilaterally declared wars, unleashed standing armies on civilians, and replaced local civil governments with martial law (regulations by a military commander over occupied territory and people). Prominent Americans confused (and continue to confuse) martial law with military law (disciplinary and punitive rules applying only to soldiers). Americans wanted a harmless army that would not impose this feared soldier's code on civilians, as Britain's army had done in Ireland, but remain instead under the rule of civil law.[1] In short, most Americans believed that liberty would be a casualty of excessive and irresponsible power, especially military power. Yet power had to exist, especially to permit adequately swift defense.

The Framers had models to avoid. Neither the unicameral Continental congresses nor the Articles of Confederation wartime national governments had resolved repetitive frictions between nation and states on civil-military relationships or evolved effective procedures to constrain martial authority. Burdened by these weights and goads, the Framers sought to keep the wielders of power accountable. They divided national work among the three branches of government in ways that were "often cryptic, ambiguous, and incomplete,"[2] especially in the ways the Constitution intertwined foreign and domestic policymaking with national and state politics.

Article I, that part of the Constitution concerned with the duties and powers of Congress, assigned to Congress a solo role in declaring wars (the Article I, section 8 authority of states to repel invasions would become a dead letter). The kind of war was not an issue at Philadelphia. Formal, declared international wars existed then, but more common then and since were undeclared conflicts between nations.[3] Article I also empowered Congress to ratify treaties and to control the purse strings for the military by limiting appropriations to two-year periods. In 1789 Jefferson especially praised this funding provision: "We have already given . . . one effectual check to the dog of war by transferring the power of letting him loose, from the executive to the legislative body, from those who are to spend to those who are to pay."[4] Congress also bore the burdens of legislating the military laws governing the organization and discipline of the armed forces; approving presidential nominees for military and civilian commissions; and holding presidents and other officials accountable by impeachment or other means. Furthermore, Congress could issue letters of marque and reprisal (these instruments of maritime retaliation became obsolete by the end of the Civil War).

Domestically, Congress (or, as it developed, the president) could suspend the habeas corpus writ privilege when, because of rebellion or invasion, the public safety required this action. Finally, Congress was to make "necessary and proper" laws to realize all of these purposes. In short, the Constitution appeared to specify congressional initiatives on foreign declared and undeclared wars and in domestic crises, as well as a presumptive claim to consultation with the president during all conflicts.

The Constitution was far more precise about the powers of Congress than about those of the president. Article II imposed on every president the following roles: commander-in-chief of the national military and of state militias when called into federal service; chief diplomat in making treaties; and major enforcer of all laws and treaties approved by Congress. Some presidents enlarged these relatively thin authorities to parallel those the Constitution assigned to Congress. "It is impossible to define with precision the scope of what we have conveniently labelled 'the President's power of martial rule,'"[5] wrote Richard Longaker in 1976.

That power has ranged from presidents assigning whole armies to fight in declared wars and in undeclared combats to repelling foreign invaders, suppressing domestic rebellions, and running military governments. Presidents have authorized tiny marine detachments of warships to punish pirates and army regiments to escort the mails in domestic strike situations and to prevent looting in national disasters. Some presidents have suspended habeas corpus, sometimes imposing martial law as well. "Just where one of these powers leaves off and the other begins is something Presidents themselves would have trouble explaining,"[6] Longaker concluded.

Presidential uses of commander-in-chief powers in wars, warlike situations, and other crises are recurring themes in American history that have often raised a countercry: force diminishes liberty. The Supreme Court, exploiting Article III, has occasionally ventured to define and even limit the war powers of the president or Congress. These rare judicial interventions were important political as well as legal-constitutional events affecting immediate public policies and prefiguring disputes about both limits on judicial review and limits on war powers.

No formal constitutional structure could insure peace abroad or stability at home. How the new government reacted to wars and emergencies would define the adequacy of the Constitution.

Early Crises, Domestic and Foreign

President Washington and the First Congress faced immediate, interacting domestic and foreign crises. Domestic strains grew out of internal taxes his administration imposed on various goods, including whiskey. When resistance to the tax grew, especially in the Pittsburgh area, Congress in 1792 enacted a militia law that authorized the president to call state militias into federal service when combinations occurred against national laws or when states could not control disorders and requested federal intervention. In mid-1794 federal judges in Pennsylvania and state governors requested national aid. Washington federalized 13,000 state militiamen, briefly and nominally served as both commander-in-chief and chief field commander, and overawed the protesters. A few endured treason trials, but Washington pardoned those found guilty. The new nation had successfully met its first domestic emergency.

The fledgling nation also had to face the increasing possibility of threats from abroad. Revolution in France in 1789 developed into a world war between France and England that would last until 1815. Although a 1778 treaty allied the United States with France, Washington's Cabinet unanimously advised neutrality, which he proclaimed unilaterally. Critics insisted that only Congress could declare war, and therefore peace. A historic debate exploded in state legislatures and in the newspapers, the latter featuring as adversaries Alexander Hamilton and James Madison, co-Framers of the Constitution and coauthors of the *Federalist Papers.* Hamilton expanded the elastic concepts of *Federalist* No. 23 and his famous implied-powers arguments on the federal bank, war debt, and tariff, asserting that a president necessarily possessed discretion in implementing treaties as well as in negotiating them. Madison argued that if a treaty negotiation risked war, a president should convene Congress for prior consultation.

In 1794 a proposed commercial treaty with England (authored by John Jay) reawakened fears of a runaway executive. The House of Representatives demanded that Washington submit all papers concerning the treaty. He refused, insisting that the House had no role to play in treaties. As a result, representatives organized a Republican party (forerunner of the present Democratic party) largely on Jefferson's strict constructionist positions, refusing at first to appropriate funds to implement the treaty, but later agreeing to the allocation.

Washington, with Federalist congressmen of Hamiltonian attitudes, had carved in the infant Constitution a view of executive initiatives amounting almost to presidential autonomy in both foreign and domestic crises, unless Congress responded negatively. Concurrently, an enduring tradition had begun, in which officials could exploit or even create emergencies in order to accumulate public support for abrasive policies, funds for pet agencies such as the armed services, and influence for themselves.

Revolutionary France, an erstwhile ally, generated extreme pressures in response to the American treaty with Britain. French warships and privateers harassed American merchantmen until an undeclared quasi war developed in 1797-1800 between the two mismatched nations. Congress funded a new navy, which successfully protected trade and seamen. Meanwhile, President John Adams outfitted merchantmen with cannon, obtaining prior agreement from Congress. The Supreme Court, in *Bas v. Tingy* (1800) and *Talbot v. Seaman* (1801), sustained Congress's rights to declare a general war and to consent to the waging of a limited war. The Court also asserted, in *Little v. Barreme* (1804), that military officers, even when obeying a president's orders during an undeclared war and misconstruing those orders, were personally accountable for damages inflicted on genuine neutrals. In short, the Constitution governed even in crises, and it allowed the president large discretion in undeclared foreign intervention, *if* Congress was consulted, even after the fact.

In decades to come, presidents would enjoy substantial autonomy in assigning navy, marine, and army units to scores of obscure, inexpensive, flag-showing interventions abroad and on America's frontiers. Such assignments, common to all maritime powers, included protecting or ransoming kidnapped merchants, shipwrecked seamen, and missionaries from pirates, border bandits, or abusive "natives"; encouraging trade and science; and recapturing fugitive slaves, even across international boundaries. In a period of uncertain and slow communications, small-unit commanders required wide discretion. Few Americans were concerned about the casualties suffered by professional military personnel in distant territories, and even less so about the fates of outlaws or natives. Soon Manifest Destiny concepts, in both America and Europe, glamorized these costs as necessary sacrifices to progress.

There was less concord about domestic, French-inspired subversion. Some outraged Americans wanted to use the army against pro-French citizens. Instead, Congress enacted the 1799 Logan Act, which prevented private citizens from corresponding with foreign governments about official American policies, and the more notorious Alien and Sedition Acts. The Alien Friends Act, which applied in both war and peace, empowered the president to arrest and deport aliens engaged in "treasonable or secret machinations,"[7] without even the thin procedural safeguards prevailing in federal and state courts. The Sedition Act, aimed at dissident American citizens, outlawed many forms of opposition to or criticism of national laws or officials, echoing, if somewhat restrainedly, England's common law of seditious libel.

Federalists insisted that the Constitution's "necessary and proper" clause incorporated the common-law standard; that the First Amendment forbade only prior restraint on oral or written political communication, not punishment for past speeches or writings; and that, unlike individual libel in which the truth of a criticism was adequate defense, the libeler of a public figure could not hide behind the truth. Furthermore, Federalists noted that the states punished seditious libels, though state bills of rights paralleled the First Amendment.

Democrats opposed these measures. Seditious libel prosecutions were both partisan persecutions masquerading as legal prosecutions (an argument given force by the venom of federal judge Samuel Chase's instructions to juries about the law of libel in Sedition Act proceedings) and inappropriate forums for American political discourse. The Sedition

Act offended the First Amendment, argued the Virginia and Kentucky resolutions, authored by Madison and Jefferson, respectively. Their concerns were for both individual liberties and state-centered federalism. If a federal common law of crimes existed, then, by analogy with Parliament, Congress could legislate on anything that came before the judges. Diverse federalism would then give way to a centralized unity, as in England. This position led to the argument that state antisedition statutes and common law should monopolize crime and punishment.

The Virginia and Kentucky resolutions were successful appeals in the 1800 election. Jefferson's new administration tried to realize its supporters' vision of a simple agrarian republic in which legislators led the executive, but Europe's continuing wars blurred this vision. After his policies became targets of Federalist journalists, Jefferson remained silent when states prosecuted journalists under state libel statutes or common law and when a federal attorney initiated a seditious libel prosecution against a vexatious critic. Jefferson's administration, however, halted the lurch toward smothering political opposition by justifying federal criminal prosecutions under the claim of emergency.

Though earlier a critic of Federalist increases of the armed services and of Adams's undeclared naval war against France, Jefferson responded to reports of the Barbary states' seizure of American ships and sailors by reinforcing the navy and sending marines to the shores of Tripoli. (This was done in close concert with Congress.) He reduced the size of the regular army, but left undisturbed the Federalist pattern of a national regular force augmentable by militia and volunteers in emergencies.

The British navy continued to impress American merchant sailors for its warships, claiming that the men were deserters and that British citizenship was inalienable. When the HMS *Leopard* attacked the American warship *Chesapeake,* Jefferson resorted to a rare solo use of emergency powers by purchasing and disbursing arms and supplies without prior statute or consultation. Congress sustained his actions by appropriating funds and, beginning in 1807, by enacting economic retaliation statutes (embargo acts), which barred exports to warring nations whose navies harassed American commerce. Federalists criticized the embargo acts as domestic coercion that exceeded, in the pursuit of foreign policies, what the Constitution allowed; but federal district judges held that it was up to Congress to regulate commerce as it saw fit, and that the search-and-seizure enforcement procedures of the embargo acts did not violate the Fourth Amendment.

Violations of the embargo acts became widespread on the long border with Canada. Jefferson, having encouraged Congress to enact a law in 1807 authorizing him to use the military in such situations, proclaimed that an insurrection existed against the enforcement of an embargo act in the

Northeast. He ordered soldiers to arrest violators of the embargo acts. Overeager federal attorneys initiated prosecutions for treason against several arrested embargo act violators. Supreme Court Justice Brockholst Livingston decided, in *U.S. v. Hoxie* (1808), that in peacetime even forcible resistance to federal law did not fit the Constitution's definition of treason, reaffirming a view Chief Justice Marshall had advanced in the Burr conspiracy trial.

Former vice-president Aaron Burr, since leaving office, had allegedly conspired with American and foreign officials to detach the new Louisiana Purchase region from the Union. Jefferson ordered General James Wilkinson to the region and on thin evidence proclaimed the existence of a treasonable conspiracy. Wilkinson arrested Burr and others and, though not imposing martial law, refused to honor habeas corpus writs issued by local judges on behalf of the prisoners. Wilkinson would have suspended civilian authority altogether, but Jefferson repudiated this swollen view of emergency prerogatives. Meanwhile, Burr was transported as a prisoner to Virginia, where he appeared before Marshall. In 1807 Marshall released Burr because the government had not shown adequate evidence of criminal action. In subsequent litigation *(Ex parte Bollman and Swartwout),* the Supreme Court decided that suspending the habeas writ was a congressional monopoly. Perhaps this view reflects the prevailing opinion that only if all normal procedures for security and justice were exhausted might martial law, then confused with military law, supersede. The ultimately futile prosecutions probably had the happy effect of preventing the use of treason trials as political weapons in real or manufactured nonwar emergencies.

The War of 1812

Formal, declared war against England in 1812 raised enduring questions about President James Madison's means and ends in encouraging Congress to the point of a war declaration.[8] The war transformed loose constructionist, nationalist Federalists, especially in New England, into fervent states' rightists. At Hartford in 1814-15 New England Federalists demanded a two-thirds vote by both houses of Congress for war declarations (thus insuring a regional veto power), an end to the three-fifths clause advantage that favored the slave-owning South in the House, and a one-term limit for presidents. Federalists justified their switch to states' rights by pointing to the diminution of state and individual rights they claimed had occurred during wartime.

Were these Federalist charges justified? True, the war declaration automatically invoked the 1798 Alien Enemies Act, and Congress had enacted another law authorizing Madison to deport enemy aliens. Secretary of State James Monroe had ordered federal marshals to list enemy aliens, yet when an enemy alien petitioned the Pennsylvania Supreme Court for a habeas corpus writ to relieve him from obedience to the federal rule, a state judge allowed the writ. The federal law could not diminish the jurisdiction of a state judge over a state resident, the judge insisted; civilians, even if enemy aliens, were not subject to military law. They *were* the proper concern of the nation during a war, and therefore the Englishman was returned to the control of the federal marshal. On circuit in Virginia, Chief Justice Marshall decided in an 1813 appeal that the Englishman should be discharged because the federal marshal had not followed procedures. The peace treaty in 1815 ended these flimsy security procedures concerning enemy aliens.[9]

During the war the nation initiated thirteen treason prosecutions against American citizens. Grand juries indicted eleven men, but trial juries acquitted them. A military court claimed jurisdiction over an American who had migrated to Canada and during the war had returned to New York, where a court-martial sentenced him to death as a spy. Madison decided that the prisoner was not subject to the jurisdiction of the military court. A South Carolina man refused to obey the president's order to mobilize in his state's militia, whereupon he was tried by a court-martial of his unit. A state judge freed the objector, deciding that the man had never become a soldier. As these cases demonstrate, the idea grew firmer that military law did not apply to civilians.

Trade regulations helped to suppress commerce with enemy areas, especially in Canada and the West Indies. Federal indictments in Vermont alone numbered more than two hundred. There might have been more, but the overburdened revenue officers were fearful of damage suits and suffered physical assaults. In early 1814 Congress responded to their complaints by enacting a revenue and trade-control law that authorized Treasury officers, marshals' posses, and soldiers to stop and search persons, buildings, or vehicles. If federal enforcement officers were sued for damages in state courts (where judges, court officers, and juries allegedly favored plaintiffs), they could shift jurisdiction to a federal district court. These provisions, some of which could potentially violate the protections specified in federal and state constitutions, did not go into effect. A treaty was signed with Britain, ending the war.

Before news of peace could circulate, General Andrew Jackson, preparing for a British attack in distant New Orleans, invoked martial law and defined civilians as soldiers for the duration of the emergency. After defeating the British in New Orleans, Jackson disregarded rumors that a treaty of peace existed and kept militia units in federal service. He arrested as spies a hostile state senator, a critical journalist, and the federal judge who had issued him a habeas corpus writ. Finally receiving official news of the peace treaty, Jackson released his prisoners. The judge immediately summoned him for contempt. Jackson appeared for the hearing but refused to reply to the charges. The judge fined him $1000 (in 1844 Congress remitted the fine with interest).

Other jurists sustained the discretionary powers of Congress and the president to decide when a crisis existed adequate to justify calling out the militia. Justice Joseph Story, in *Martin v. Mott* (1827), offered this classic support not only for the elastic nature of emergency powers, but also for the presence of democratic checks on these powers:

> The power thus confided by Congress to the President is doubtless of a very high and delicate nature. A free people are naturally very jealous of the exercise of military power; and the power to call the militia into actual service is certainly felt to be one of no ordinary magnitude. . . . It is, in its terms, a limited power, confined to cases of actual invasion, or of imminent danger of invasion. If it be a limited power, the question arises, by whom is the exigency to be judged of and decided? . . . We are all of opinion that the authority to decide whether the exigency has arisen belongs exclusively to the President, and that his decision is conclusive upon all other persons. . . . It is no answer that such a power may be abused, for there is no power which is not susceptible of abuse. The remedy for this, as well as for all other misconduct, if it should occur, is to be found in the constitution itself. In a free government the danger must be remote, since in addition to the high qualities which the Executive must be presumed to possess, of public virtue and honest devotion to the public interests, the frequency of elections and the watchfulness of the representatives of the nation, carry with them all the checks which can be useful to guard against usurpation and wanton tyranny.[10]

Though the War of 1812 could have opened the door for capricious and vicious attacks on both alien residents and citizen dissenters, the United States' efforts to achieve internal security were mild by contemporary foreign standards; Jackson's arbitrary orders were the most severe. Prosecutions under law (however ill-advised the particular law), rather than lawless persecutions, marked the conduct of the American government when dealing with both troops and civilians. In light of the United States' sad military record during the war, remarkable respect was shown to constitutional operations, legal procedures, and the laws of war. Federally and democratically organized constitutional government, even in a relatively weak and divided nation caught up in world revolution and war, had coped decently with both internal and foreign crises.

The record to 1815 suggests that recent concepts of constitutional dictatorship, that is, that democracies must surrender control of power to authoritarian executives in crises, are not completely applicable to this period. Jefferson, though exaggerating the degree of crisis presented by Burr's intrigues, had employed Lockean ideas of the duty of the government to preserve itself beyond constitutional limits; yet a high degree of accountability for crisis policies existed in the form of open democratic processes and other forums for redress, such as elections and courts. The goal of emergency doctrines was adequately powerful democracy, rather than government enfeebled by exaggerated discordances among its separate branches. Distinctions were large between actual policies and constitutional-legal doctrines of war and emergency powers. Presidents, legislators, and judges were traveling roughly parallel paths in emergencies, reaching reasonable destinations while avoiding confrontations. If presidents used emergency power in a sweeping manner, no one president had claimed a unilateral right to initiate substantial military actions or had suggested that Congress lacked capacities to limit executive conduct. These were sound foundations on which to define the postwar nation when, at last, Europe's turmoils could be omitted from the definition.[11]

II

Testing War Powers, 1815-1865

Struggles for a Balance of Power

Foreign wars and domestic strains tested further whether the diverse, dispersing society could hold together. In 1819, 1822, and 1826 Congress enacted piracy acts, which authorized navy commanders to seize pirates and bring them to justice, presumably under international law. Monroe's dramatic doctrine of 1823, which seemed to immunize the Americas against further European colonization by casting the United States as the continent's lone police, pleased those who favored presidential initiatives in diplomacy. Domestically, Henry Clay redefined the republican Constitution in loose constructionist terms as an "American system" in which tariffs, a national bank, subsidized national roads, and other internal improvements would sustain more adequate armed forces.[1]

Congress enacted major elements of Clay's package, but by the early 1830s his purposes hit sectionalist rocks and constitutional shoals. South Carolina's John C. Calhoun, fearing that the 1828 tariff would undermine the slave economy, escalated states' rights into state sovereignty, insisting that the "original" Constitution was a contract between the states and that the tariff law was unconstitutional. South Carolina nullified the tariff law and instructed the governor to enforce its action with militia. At President Jackson's urging, Congress enacted a Force Act in 1833, which authorized federal judges to issue writs against noncomplying state officers. (Earlier, federal writs could be issued only against national officials.) Another political compromise defused this crisis of federalism but diminished neither Calhoun's fears nor Jackson's perceptions of presidential stewardship as the special guardian of national interests in emergencies.

Successive Supreme Court justices and attorneys general advanced a doctrine that the "take care" clause of the Constitution imposed on the president the duty to exert the nation's total power, not that of the executive alone. In the absence of contrary statutes, the Court decided in 1818 that a president had a common-law right to sue on behalf of the nation in commercial disputes. *American Insurance Company v. Canter* (1825) sustained the nation's power to acquire territories by conquest or purchase and to regulate these territories, and *Martin v. Mott* (1827) upheld a wartime president's discretionary right to judge the level of emergency necessary to federalize state militias. Furthermore, judges virtually immunized executive officers from damage lawsuits, thus lessening accountability.

Legal doctrines did not, however, translate immediately into White House policies. Jackson obtained congressional approval before retaliating against Argentinian commerce raiders and seizing French maritime property in lieu of a French debt. John Quincy Adams, then a representative in Congress, successfully defended Jackson's craggy diplomacy with the French as having been arrived at after adequate consultation with Congress. Although Congress agreed, it also stipulated that it was not delegating to Jackson the solo power to declare war. Adams later argued that the Constitution recognized both declared and undeclared wars. He pointed out that presidents since Washington had sent troops into many nonwar combats (but Adams did not note that these involved obscure places, private offenders, small numbers of troops, and trivial consequences). In the 1840s he added his developing antislavery views to those he held on the Constitution's capacity to reach individuals in states, even to the extent of abolishing state-recognized private property.

Texas shaped such notions in the crucible of politics. Jackson and his immediate successors, Democrat Martin Van Buren and Whig William Henry Harrison, refrained from pressing the question of U.S. annexation of Texas, but when President John Tyler shifted from Whig to Democratic allegiance, he set out to annex the slaveholding Republic of Texas. Tyler and his otherwise strict constructionist administration (Calhoun had been named secretary of state) won congressional approval for annexation by joint resolution, which required only a majority vote in both houses. This action avoided the two-thirds Senate vote required for treaties and linked the House to diplomacy, yet gave the president a lever in foreign affairs to bring Congress to a declaration of war. Succeeding Tyler, President James Polk ordered troops to the disputed Mexico-Texas border, where firefights began. Congress then "recognized" the existence of war between the United States and Mexico.

Whigs and some Democrats bitterly denounced the president's maneuvering. Illinois Whig Representative Abraham Lincoln, for example, rejected Polk's plea of necessity as justification for ordering American regulars to the unstable borderland without prior consultation with Congress, which Lincoln believed distorted commander-in-chief into war powers. "Allow the president to invade a neighboring nation, whenever he shall deem it necessary to repel an invasion . . . and you allow him to make war at his pleasure," Lincoln wrote. The Framers, he continued, had wrought the Constitution so that ". . . no man should hold the power of bringing this oppression upon us."[2] A House resolution implied that Polk had overextended the commander-in-chief power, but as a whole, Congress avoided the issue of presidential prestructuring of an American war declaration.

Whigs also attacked Polk as a dictatorial usurper of the war powers when he authorized military governments in Mexico without Congress's prior assent. Whigs rejected the Democratic view that a president's authority to create military governments was implicit in the Constitution. In the 1850s American judges, deciding lawsuits arising from the military government in Mexico, sustained American commanders. They did so on the basis of the idea, expressed in James Kent's *Commentaries on American Law* (1826) and increasingly accepted, that a successful military commander occupying a defeated belligerent's territory became military governor and assumed the authority of the displaced sovereign. Operating without statute, this authority issued in martial law, under which military commissions could try and punish civilian guerillas, looters, saboteurs, and spies. These decisions helped to diffuse further among lawyers the Lockean idea that government possessed a basic right to self-defense in genuine crises. Anticipatory impositions of martial law, like injunctions to thwart civil evils, were, however, all but unthinkable. Legal authorities also agreed that martial law should not be a vehicle to shape civil government but one to preserve order, and that it should always be a last resort.

The 1842 Dorr War in Rhode Island and the derivative *Luther v. Borden* decision (1849) in the Supreme Court kept confusions alive and affected legal and constitutional thought on war and emergency powers. Rhode Islanders who benefited from existing arrangements refused to democratize voting and tax standards by revising the state's antique constitution (which was essentially the 1663 charter). Frustrated reformers, calling themselves Dorrites after the leading protester, Thomas Dorr, created their own constitutional revision and elected officials. Incumbent authorities declined to recognize the reformers and called out the militia, which under martial law arrested and tried hundreds of resisters in special nonjudicial tribunals. In short, Rhode Island applied martial law to civilians in an anticipatory manner, in order to shape the civil government. When the Dorrites realized that President Tyler favored the charter authorities, the rebellion collapsed.

Which contending state government was legitimate? Congress, by inaction, had left that decision to the president. Just after the Mexican War victory in 1849, the Supreme Court, speaking through Chief Justice Roger B. Taney in *Luther v. Borden,* also refused to answer this "political question." Taney justified the Court's hands-off, political-question stance in *Luther* by asking if a court were the proper forum in which to determine whether a president decided correctly to federalize state militias:

> If the judicial power extends so far, the guarantee [of a republican form of government] contained in the Constitution of the United States is a guarantee of anarchy, and not of order. . . . It is said that this power in the President is dangerous to liberty, and may be abused. All

> power may be abused if placed in unworthy hands. . . . When citizens of the same State are in arms against each other, and the constituted authorities unable to execute the laws, the interposition of the United States must be prompt, or it is of little value. The ordinary course of proceedings in courts of justice would be utterly unfit for the crisis. And the elevated office of the President, chosen as he is by the people of the United States, and the high responsibility he could not fail to feel when acting in a case of so much moment, appear to furnish as strong safeguards against a wilful abuse of power as human prudence and foresight could well provide. At all events, it is conferred upon him by the Constitution and laws of the United States, and must therefore be respected and enforced in its judicial tribunals.[3]

In governing, nondecisions are decisions. The *Luther* decision meant that the incumbent Rhode Island government had won in the highest legal forum, which spread the idea that a state had a right to self-defense, including the use of martial law, akin to the nation's in various emergencies including slave insurrections, worker strikes, urban riots, and cholera epidemics. Lawyers expanded Taney's *Luther* doctrine that governments facing allegedly serious crises could impose martial law, and by the mid-1850s Attorney General Caleb Cushing suggested that American martial law could equal the French *état de siege,* an indefinitely prolonged condition of emergency in which civil protections disappear. This extraordinary suggestion did not become policy, however, even during the Civil War and Reconstruction.

The Civil War

The problems of war making and military government increased exponentially when the Confederate States of America, a government formed after the secession of seven Deep South states, bombarded the Union's Fort Sumter in South Carolina in April 1861. What *were* appropriate and constitutional responses to state secessions in 1860-61, and then to a civil war that became the Western world's longest, most costly conflict since Napoleon's surrender? Here was no popgun Whiskey Rebellion or single-state nullification. A discredited United States government faced hostile armies in a vast arc from the Potomac to Texas. Pro-secession activists infested critical areas in slaveholding border states and in some free states. Federal and state criminal laws became irrelevant or uncertain.

President Lincoln transformed northern outrage into militarily relevant and constitutionally and politically supportable emergency policies. He employed all available crisis doctrines, especially those concerning the president's prerogatives in either declared or undeclared foreign wars and the innate self-defense duty the Constitution imposed on the nation. But Lincoln would not accept the argument that a president possessed emergency powers independent of both the Constitution and Congress and refused to impose the European *état de siege*.

In civil wars abroad, few officials needed constitutional justifications for coercive policies, but Americans felt an inescapable need to have constitutional positions on such matters as the right of the nation militarily to resist state secessions, to frustrate pro-secession individuals and groups in unseceded states (and later in conquered parts of the South), and to rebuild state and local governments. Lincoln's "dogmas from the quiet past" had to be applied, a conviction that inspired self-proclaimed constitutional experts to review Grotius and Vattel, the Dorr Rebellion, and the American military government experience in Mexico. Lincoln's administration applied these and other precedents in the Civil War's vaster scale and duration in an eventually constructive, moderate, and responsible manner.[4]

The first Lincoln policy was the arbitrary arrest of civilians by soldiers acting on the commander-in-chief's orders, sometimes involving habeas corpus suspensions. The second was the blockade of southern ports and the punishment of evaders of Treasury and navy wartime controls. The third, military Reconstruction of states, began as informal local belligerent occupations, which first ascended to statewide military governments and then escalated to state Reconstruction, including the emancipation of slaves.

Arbitrary arrests became a central constitutional issue within days after Sumter's surrender. In Maryland Union soldiers arrested and jailed prominent pro-Confederate activist John Merryman but permitted him access to his family's lawyer (globally the rarest privilege in civil wars, yet one that became the norm in the United States). Merryman's attorney brought in Chief Justice Taney from Washington. With unprecedented advance notice to journalists, Taney, himself a Marylander, convened in Baltimore a special session of his circuit court and issued a habeas writ. Lincoln ordered Merryman's jailers to ignore it, whereupon Taney publicly savaged the president for destroying civil justice. Taney insisted that the federal habeas writ had always protected all Americans (it had rarely been significant previously) and that only Congress could suspend it. Confusing martial law with military law, and bypassing his own political-question *Luther* doctrine, Taney concluded wrongly that the Constitution fettered all warlike powers until Congress formally declared war.

Lincoln avoided the direct clash that Taney invited. He responded instead through messages to Congress, pointing to precedents (especially Taney's judgments in *Luther*) that had sustained executive initiatives and government self-defense. Lincoln stressed the entire nation's constitutional capacity, rather than competition between separate branches. Meanwhile, antiwar Democrats, exploiting the *Merryman* decision, disassociated themselves from secession and applied their traditional negative economic positions to internal security and blockade policies and later to conscription, emancipation, and state Reconstruction. Democrats rediscovered the Bill of Rights (for whites only), extolled states' rights, and insisted that only Congress could unleash the war powers. "King Linkum" was a dictator, therefore, a charge heard again in the wartime Supreme Court when the justices, in *Ex parte Vallandigham* (1864), refused jurisdiction of an appeal from a defeated Democratic congressman from Ohio whom the army had arrested, tried, and convicted for disloyalty.

Lawyers for violators of Lincoln's blockade orders, the second emergency policy, denied Lincoln's constitutional right to close American ports, even those held by rebels, because no declared war existed. This issue came to the Supreme Court in the 1863 *Prize* cases. A bare majority of the justices affirmed Lincoln's position that a civil war was not a declared war and that the president had the duty to decide when and how to resist mass insurrection and disloyalty.

Lincoln's policies on military government, emancipation, and state Reconstruction in the occupied South were developed because from the beginning of the war he had extralegally sustained anti-secessionists in Virginia, Maryland, and Missouri with funds and arms, and because Union forces kept enlarging areas of control in Secessia. Nineteenth-century nations generally agreed that even in declared international wars, only the will of victorious commanders (the president, for the United States) defined belligerent occupations. In civil wars these gossamer reins did not exist. Lincoln and Congress gradually won control over the Union generals' discordant policies in belligerent occupations and therefore made possible civilian control of military government, emancipation (including the arming of blacks), and state Reconstruction policies.

Union occupation of an area created many political problems. Desiring to use the Confederacy's labor force, many Union soldiers evaded the orders of some generals to enforce the 1850 Fugitive Slave Act, which required the return of runaway blacks to their owners, even if Confederate. Occupying troops often decided which whites should hold office, witness in trials, contract, and vote. Such political choices by troops aided the paths to both emancipation and state Reconstruction, but Lincoln and Republican party leaders determined the shape and pace of these policies, thereby encouraging visions of a reconstructed southern society.

Congress shared Lincoln's views on the evils of slavery and the need for military suppression of slavery. Congress repealed the Fugitive Slave Act and passed confiscation acts in 1861 and 1862, which required individual prosecutions of disloyal persons before their human property could be freed. Potentially more wide-reaching in its effect was Lincoln's unilateral Emancipation Proclamation, a commander-in-chief order of September

1862. When it took effect on January 1, 1863, Lincoln stipulated that the Union's armies would henceforth recruit black soldiers; thus, the South would supply manpower for its own demise.

Military Reconstruction was also based on the commander-in-chief powers in a civil war. In mid-1862 Lincoln appointed a military governor for Tennessee, an office presidents had heretofore employed only briefly when administering conquered foreign areas or thinly populated new American territories after their purchase or conquest. He chose Andrew Johnson for the position. Johnson had been the only senator from a seceding state to reject secession and had been forced to flee to Washington in 1861. He returned to Tennessee in the wake of Union troops as both military governor and general, with orders to rebuild loyal authority. Rigorous in suppressing active disloyalty through arbitrary arrests, loyalty tests, and banishments, Johnson upset property rights as little as possible while accepting the military need for emancipation.[5]

By late 1862 Lincoln had become converted to the abolitionist belief that the Union would always be in peril unless slavery's destabilizing influences were ended. Employing the war powers, Lincoln proclaimed a general military Reconstruction policy for the still defiant South on December 8, 1863. Union military governors were to revive civil government and statewide political processes in occupied Secessia and initiate constitutional conventions in which voters had to provide for emancipation. Lincoln dared to espouse "only" emancipation at this time, not biracial voting or officeholding. He also acknowledged that Congress need not recognize representatives of reconstructed states and that the Supreme Court might reverse emancipation, among other war powers policies.[6]

All emergency war powers and policies were debated in calendared presidential and state elections in 1862 and 1864. Democratic spokesmen contrasted Lincoln's Civil War actions with his rejection in 1848 of Polk's justifications for ordering American soldiers to fight in Mexico. But in 1848 Lincoln had been commenting on an international conflict, not on an undeclarable civil war. In 1861 the nation was not invading a foreign land but defending itself, a right that constitutional theorists had claimed since the 1690s. Lincoln had "no choice but to call out the war power of the Government."[7] This absence of alternatives led him to join war and commander-in-chief powers, greatly enlarging the concept and practice of presidential crisis stewardship.

The ratification of his policies by voters and Congress undergirded Lincoln's admonition to Congress in December 1863 never to forget that the war powers remained the Union's "main reliance." He had come to the White House with dynamic views on emergency doctrines, if in relatively unsophisticated form, and had communicated them ably to his citizens. These concepts guided him to the Constitution's scattered war powers clauses and to the president's oath of office. Lincoln found authority to resist secessions and active disloyalty in seceded or unseceded states and to reorganize the latter while remaining accountable to voters and litigants through elections and lawsuits. Regarding the Constitution as an organic source of power adequate for all necessary public purposes, he accepted the difficult duty of controlling the numerous military and civilian officials who, in his name, exercised the nation's war powers in a civil war that Congress had allowed to be a largely presidential war.

Lincoln never fought with Congress. Instead, he cooperated usefully with lawmakers, especially those controlling appropriations, commissions, and promotions, to keep civilians in control of the military. The three-part balance among the federal government's branches remained viable, although Lincoln did greatly enhance the presidency. Lincoln never imposed his will on Congress, except through the traditional arts of patronage and persuasion. Despite criticism from far-right Democrats and some Republicans, Congress approved all of Lincoln's war powers expedients.

Tensions did exist between the White House and Capitol Hill on such issues as Lincoln's pocket-veto of the 1864 Wade-Davis Bill, Republican lawmakers' own version of military Reconstruction. That year, despite this intraparty strain, the Republicans and "War" Democrats renominated and then reelected Lincoln, the first second-term president since Jackson. In short, by 1864 all the governing and political institutions of the nation were working in adequate, if fragile, harmony. By 1865 shared support existed not only for the Thirteenth Amendment (which contrasted sharply with an earlier Thirteenth Amendment proposal that would have unamendably guaranteed that the nation would never interfere with slaveholders' rights in existing states) but also for the Freedmen's Bureau, the nation's first statutory administrative agency.

It is notable that as the Civil War drew to a close, although a Sedition Act disgraced the statute books, it remained unenforced. No mass executions, exilings, property confiscations, or disfranchisements (all common practices in civil wars abroad) occurred. Military emancipation and state Reconstruction were directed toward increasing the number of voters and returning the seceded states to participation in the federal Union with enhanced voting power, once the three-fifths clause was eliminated. Instead of law falling silent during the Civil War, novel questions of constitutional legal rights tested the Constitution's significance in emergencies as never before. State-based, two-party politics, expressed in calendared elections and constitutional amendments, helped to shape military policy, and federalism grew stronger.

Lincoln sometimes doubted the capacity of constitutional democracy to survive the Civil War. In April 1864, in a private letter, he described a president's wartime powers as a duty less to observe any technical definition of executive war powers than one to preserve the Constitution, the government, and the nation for which the Constitution existed "by every indispensable means." Should the nation be lost, the Constitution, the "organic law," would also die. "I felt that measures, otherwise unconstitutional, might become lawful, by becoming indispensable to the preservation of the [C]onstitution through the preservation of the nation. Right or wrong, I assumed this ground, and now avow it."[8]

This statement can be misconstrued as a self-admission that he was a constitutional dictator, a label employed by both nineteenth- and twentieth-century observers. Lincoln blunted the potential for presidential dictatorship by helping Congress and the courts to hold accountable those soldiers and civilians to whom he had delegated war powers, and by remaining accountable himself.

Lincoln's commitment to emancipation and the use of Negro soldiers raised fears among extreme racists that he might, after the shooting ended, continue to use not only the war powers but also the efficient concord he had developed with Congress to steer national policy toward legal equality for blacks. Indeed, on February 1, 1865 Lincoln told a happy Washington crowd that Congress's passage of the proposed Thirteenth Amendment, which abolished slavery nationwide, left a task still undone. The amendment, he said, was a "very fitting if not indispensable adjunct to winding up the great difficulty." Abolition was the essential preliminary to the "perfected" reunion of all the states, "and to attain this end it was necessary that the original disturbing cause [of the war] should . . . be rooted out." But even the Thirteenth Amendment fell "far short of what the amendment will be when fully consumated." It was ". . . a King's cure for all the evils. It winds the whole thing up."[9] On April 11, 1865, in what was to be his last public address, Lincoln stated that he was contemplating as a requirement for state restorations (deriving from the Thirteenth Amendment) political participation for at least a token number of literate Negroes and for black veterans of the Union army in the southern states; he was also leaning toward requiring that public schools in the South admit black children. Three days later, John Wilkes Booth, a passionate opponent of black citizenship and leader of a conspiracy devoted to Confederate ideals, assassinated Lincoln.

Lincoln left a legacy of both practices and theories that supported the widest latitude for uses of the war powers in genuine emergencies, yet conformed to Locke's ancient admonitions. Lincoln and Congress substantially changed the war-emergency doctrines that had been accepted since the Dorr Rebellion and the Mexican War, especially those that stressed that victorious officials should not use emergency powers in an anticipatory manner or with intent to reshape the political or social structures of a conquered belligerent.

The assassination of Lincoln, coming so close in time to the final crumpling of the Confederacy, raised a host of questions. However phrased, they tended to ask: For what purposes, for which beneficiaries, and for how long should the victor continue to exercise war and emergency powers after the shooting had ended?

III

Applying War Powers, 1865-1917

Reconstruction, whether before or after Appomattox, defined by the president or by Congress, had to be military. Only the victorious army, though swiftly dwindling and reprofessionalizing after the Confederacy's surrender, was relevant to Reconstruction tasks, if only to police the newly surrendered South.

Denying a right or need for the army even as a temporary police, ultra-right Democrats insisted that the reconquered states should automatically return to full federal relations. Equally uninfluential Radical Republicans argued that the southern states were either destroyed or reduced to territorial status, and that a substantial military occupation of the South for an indefinite period was in order, especially to sustain the legal rights of freed blacks. Both positions inspired endless, almost metaphysical arguments about the nature of a state in the Union, an abstraction that Lincoln had derided and that the Supreme Court had dodged in *Luther* as a political question. What prevailed were middle-range alternatives initiated by the new president, Andrew Johnson, under carry-over war and commander-in-chief powers. When these policies proved to be unbearably reactionary in terms of minimal rights due Americans in their states of residence, Congress initiated in 1867 its own military Reconstruction. Initially, the Supreme Court tended to support the president, as in the 1867 *Milligan* and *Test Oath* decisions. Later, in *Texas v. White* (1869), the justices sustained Congress's authority to decide what the form and purposes of a military occupation of the South should be.

Those familiar with the savagery suffered by the defeated in civil wars abroad, as in Mexico and France, were impressed that in the United States there were no mass executions, exilings, property confiscations (except for emancipation itself), or disfranchisements. Instead, Reconstruction policies, though resulting in early 1868 in the only impeachment of a president, were designed to restore the southern states as quickly as possible, to enlarge rather than diminish state electorates, and to forgive rather than punish ex-Confederates.

Military Reconstruction

No official was more experienced than Johnson at using national war powers to shape a state's political and legal standards. Notoriously rigorous as military governor of Tennessee, Johnson became Lincoln's

1864 running mate on a pro-emancipation, war-to-victory platform. Now president, Johnson first kept the army on short-range peacekeeping tasks in the South. From May through December 1865 Johnson suspended enforcement of the confiscation acts. He carried out new state Reconstruction with army aid and funds, and in none of this Reconstruction did he hold to, much less advance beyond, Lincoln's April 11, 1865 position of welcoming equal legal rights for blacks, token participation of black Union veterans as voters or officeholders, or public schools for children of both races. Instead, Johnson amnestied or pardoned thousands of ex-Confederates, including leading secessionists. Violating wartime laws that required loyalty oaths for federal officials, as well as the Freedmen's Bureau law that implemented equal legal rights for blacks, Johnson appointed provisional governors (successors to wartime military governors) and other local officials down to the humblest sheriffs responsible for justice and order, thereby reactivating Democratic party organizations.

By December the Thirteenth Amendment was ratified (very reluctantly in the ex-Confederate states), thus voiding the three-fifths clause and adding substantially to the South's numbers in the House of Representatives. In addition, the new Black Codes of a dozen Johnson states excluded freed blacks from political and legal self-protections available in other states and, arguably, violated the Thirteenth Amendment. Reliable witnesses before Congress's new standing Joint Committee on Reconstruction testified that state justice officials left violence against blacks unpunished. Johnson still insisted that Congress had to admit the South's delegations without conditions.

Congress, the sole judge of the entrance qualifications of its own members, kept the southern states from representation. Contemporary legal opinion, soon reaffirmed in *U.S. v. Rhodes* (1866) and *In re Turner* (1867), broadly defined the Thirteenth Amendment as requiring color-blind official and private behavior for state residents. To secure this minimum, Congress passed the world's first civil rights law, over Johnson's veto. This law enforced the Thirteenth Amendment and forecast the Fourteenth (which, overshadowing the Thirteenth, became misinterpreted as protecting individual rights only against official state infringements, not against private acts). The Civil Rights Act encouraged individual self-defense through lawsuits, and Congress increased federal court jurisdiction in appeals from racially prejudiced state courts. Johnson discouraged implementation of the act, however, and returning to the Democratic party, favored conservative Democratic candidates in the 1866 congressional and state elections. Voters outside the South sustained Republicans who promised to restore the ex-rebel states to representation upon ratification of the pending Fourteenth Amendment.

Two years after Appomattox, Congress overrode the president's vetoes and enacted its own military Reconstruction laws, regularizing the army's Reconstruction role that since 1861 had been defined only by executive orders. Congress based its Reconstruction laws on a "grasp of war" theory, which accepted both the existence of the conquered states and the rightfulness of the nation's (that is, Congress's) temporary martial authority over them, a view that the Supreme Court would sustain in *Texas v. White* (1869). Nevertheless, the military Reconstruction laws extended the Constitution's "normal" provisions.

The alternatives may well have been worse. Aiming not to govern states but to restore them quickly to federal relations, though now with biracial electorates, the military Reconstruction laws defined the outer limits of federal intervention for equal rights. The states themselves would end Reconstruction, after creating with army supervision at least superficially nondiscriminatory new constitutions and laws and ratifying the Fourteenth Amendment. The South, however, rejected even this tokenism.

Executing Reconstruction Act duties, Johnson appointed generals as military governors, but he obstructed their goals. His able attorney general, Henry Stanbery, circularized opinions on the effect of Johnson's declaration of peace that made army and bureau officers uncertain of the legality of military Reconstruction. The president even risked politicizing the army's officer corps by offering General W. T. Sherman command of an unauthorized army department, one perhaps meant to obey only the commander-in-chief. General Ulysses S. Grant apparently convinced Sherman to reject the dangerous bait.

Supreme Court judgments, such as Taney's *Merryman* opinion, encouraged Johnson and other conservatives. Although the *Prize* cases (1863) and the *Vallandigham* decision (1864) had sustained the blockade and internal security, the Court decided in the *Milligan* decision (1867) that the wartime military trial of an Indiana man for actively aiding the rebellion violated his rights under the Fifth and Sixth Amendments. The Constitution protected everyone, even in the midst of a titanic civil conflict, stated Justice David Davis. "No doctrine, involving more pernicious consequences, was ever invented by the wit of man than that any of its [the Constitution's] provisions can be suspended during any of the great exigencies of government."[1] Furthermore, early in 1867 the Court, by a five-to-four vote in the *Test Oath* cases, held unconstitutional the wartime federal law prescribing an oath of past loyalty for lawyers practicing on national courts and a similar oath Missouri's constitution required of licensed professionals. The *Test Oath* decisions were extraordinary enlargements of judicial review, based on novel applications of equity responsibility in the courts. Though praised as defenses of individual rights, all of these decisions actually sustained only the rights of whites and opened state courts and professions in the South and federal offices nationwide to former rebels. Thereafter, the Court hesitated to intrude further into Reconstruction policy, declining to hear appeals by southern whites in *Mississippi v. Johnson* (1867) and *Georgia v. Stanton* (1868), which alleged the unconstitutionality of the military Reconstruction laws, and in the *McCardle* case (1869), which sustained Congress's repeal of the Court's jurisdiction over one form of habeas appeal. In *Texas v. White* (1869), the Court, echoing Taney in *Luther,* held that the nation had a duty both to protect itself through legislation and to guarantee republican forms of government to the states. According to the Supreme Court, what Congress had done was constitutional, or at least not unconstitutional.

Three years after Appomattox, Johnson was still determined to control the army and perhaps to polarize issues in an election year. He ejected Secretary of War Edwin M. Stanton from that key office and tried to send Grant abroad on a trivial diplomatic mission, thereby defying laws designed to shield the secretary and general from ejection or transfer. Congress was left with two choices: either abandon its Reconstruction-as-reform commitment to set the defeated states' laws into relatively color-blind motion;[2] or check Johnson's misuses of emergency and commander-in-chief powers. The Constitution offered only an untried means: impeachment. Important scholars would later claim that the impeachment of Johnson disguised Republican desires to favor business interests, an unconvincing view. Escaping conviction by a single Senate vote, Johnson largely abandoned active opposition to Reconstruction, but he had succeeded nevertheless in swerving a society away from uncomfortably novel commitments to racial equality. Thereafter, Congress readmitted southern states, though laggards had to ratify not only the Fourteenth Amendment but also the Fifteenth, which prohibited states from denying suffrage to nonwhite males because of race, extended self-help from courts to polls, as in the Civil Rights Act, and stressed calendared elections more than emergency doctrines.

Most impediments against black voters were now set up by individuals, though state and local officials often left violence unpunished or joined unofficially in assaulting blacks. Congress, therefore, in Enforcement Acts of the early 1870s, regularized emergency interventions by federal officers by making the intimidation of voters by violence or bribery a new federal crime and by outlawing conspiracies against persons exercising constitutional rights. An 1871 Ku Klux Klan act punished individual denials of equal legal protection and due process on the theory that only state inaction allowed the growing resort to violence. Grant, now president, could suspend the habeas corpus writ and use the army against conspirators.

The shrunken professional army could not, however, patrol the vast South. Whites learned to use nonviolent intimidation. Enforcement in thousands of local communities where law and custom stubbornly opposed racial equality fatigued white America.[3] Northern opinion, accepting distorted Darwinian ideas on race, in early 1877 sanctioned a retreat from Reconstruction following the disputed presidential election of 1876.[4]

Judicial opinions helped to undercut support for racial equality. The Supreme Court's *Slaughterhouse* decision (1873) narrowly defined federal rights and the nation's responsibilities to secure them. In *U.S. v. Reese* (1876), the Court held that the Fifteenth Amendment forbade states only from withholding the vote on racial grounds, a virtual invitation for discriminatory literacy tests and manipulative residence and poll tax requirements. The *Civil Rights* cases (1883) recreated a sharply separated dual federalism in which the protectable national rights, like traveling interstate or abroad, were irrelevant to most persons. Legal textbooks, including Thomas McIntyre Cooley's long-lived *Constitutional Limitations* (1868), taught generations of paper-chasing future lawyers and judges that these were valid readings of the Constitution.

During Reconstruction Congress sought to identify the civil rights of national citizens. Abandoning emergency doctrines as quickly as possible, Congress, which even during the Civil War had never acknowledged unilateral presidential control of military power, resorted to constitutional amendments and enforcement statutes that used courts and the army as implementing institutions. Andrew Johnson had not favored equal rights for blacks, and the Supreme Court had proved to be unsympathetic; even so, the Court never decided against military Reconstruction.

Crises in Labor

Between 1877 and 1914 domestic crises centered on class more than on race. The presidency lost its character as the nation's steward, in part because of prejudiced military interventions in labor-management disputes. Presidents justified these interventions by using distorted emergency doctrines.

In 1877 governors requested military aid from President Rutherford B. Hayes to control labor violence against the railroads, which some Cabinet members equated with treason. When strikers disobeyed court orders, Hayes declared martial law on railroad rights-of-way and ordered soldiers to keep the lines open. Judges created a form of preventive emergency doctrine to justify injunctions against strikers. The army became a posse for marshals and sheriffs, a development that reformers tried to curtail in the 1878 Posse Comitatus Act by restricting uses of the military by peace officers or private persons, as in labor disputes.

President Grover Cleveland's administration, the first Democratic one since Buchanan's, had to deal with the crisis that resulted when in 1894 Jacob Coxey led an "army" of unemployed people in the commandeering of the cars of bankrupt railroads in receivership. Cleveland's Attorney General

Richard Olney supported the requests of governors for federal troops, but Cleveland temporized. When Coxey was arrested for walking on the Capitol lawn, the crisis evaporated.

Subsequent strikes against the Pullman Car Company escalated until violence blocked Chicago, the nation's rail hub. Olney believed that the president possessed inherent authority to keep communications open and obtained from federal district judges an omnibus injunction against the strikers' union, which was led by Eugene Debs. The injunction barred interference with rail-borne mails and interstate commerce. Although interferences continued, Illinois governor John P. Altgeld insisted that federal troops were unnecessary; but Cleveland, misled by Olney, sent soldiers and five thousand deputy marshals, who broke the strike and arrested Debs. Upon his conviction, Debs appealed to the Supreme Court. In the historic *In re Debs* decision (1895), Justice David Brewer sustained the conviction, insisting that the nation had a broad constitutional duty to protect mails and commerce, even against contrary state policies or private rights. The *Debs* decision linked government more to selfish interests than to national self-protection in emergencies and gave credence to the claims of ideological radicals that emergency doctrines merely camouflaged the interests of capitalists.

Presidents of the early twentieth century, by limiting partisan uses of emergency powers in domestic labor disputes, improved the nation's constitutional stance. Violent strikes in Pennsylvania coal fields brought President Theodore Roosevelt to new frontiers of intervention. Readying federal troops when governors requested aid, Roosevelt made it clear that soldiers were not to be police for employers. In 1903 he refused to send troops requested by Colorado's governor to break a miners' strike. Roosevelt dispatched troops to a Nevada strike in 1907 but enforced their neutrality. In 1914, when women and children died in a massacre apparently committed by an antilabor Colorado militia during a mining strike, President Woodrow Wilson agreed to the governor's request for federal troops only after authorizing the federal troops to disregard state habeas writs and ordering the governor to withdraw the uncontrollable militia.

Crises in Diplomacy

In militant diplomacy, Congress, though edgy about Johnson's initiatives in Reconstruction and the 1867 purchase of Alaska, allowed the president a fairly free rein, especially if Americans abroad allegedly suffered kidnapping or other abuses. A July 1868 law provided that:

> Whenever it is made known to the President that any citizen of the United States has been unjustly deprived of his liberty by or under the authority of any foreign government, it shall be the duty of the

> President forthwith to demand of that government the reasons of such imprisonment; and if it appears to be wrongful and in violation of the rights of American citizenship, the President shall forthwith demand the release of such citizen, and if the release so demanded is unreasonably delayed or refused, the President shall use such means, not amounting to acts of war, as he may think necessary and proper to obtain or effectuate the release; and all the facts and proceedings relative thereto shall as soon as practicable be communicated by the President to Congress.[5]

On the other hand, Congress frustrated Grant's project to annex Santo Domingo in 1870. Lawmakers again participated in diplomacy in the late 1870s with a Chinese immigration restriction bill (which violated a treaty) and in the 1890s with joint resolutions condemning attacks on Christians in Turkey. The Supreme Court's *Whitney v. Robertson* decision (1888), to the effect that a law and a treaty were of equal stature, appeared to approve of Congress as a diplomatic partner to the president, but Congress only infrequently asserted such claims against presidents in foreign policies. Presidents of the 1865-1917 period unilaterally revived the Monroe Doctrine, discouraged French empire building in Mexico, and by 1890 contrived for the United States a naval base in the Kingdom of Hawaii and shared rule of Samoa with England and Germany.

In 1898 a declared war over Cuba broke out between Spain and the United States. By its end, American troops dominated nearby Cuba and Puerto Rico, distant Hawaii and Guam, and the even more distant Philippines. With no further authority than the war declaration, President William McKinley assigned 125,000 American soldiers to suppress Philippine nationalists and added substantial American forces to an international expedition against antiforeign Boxer rebels in China, which led China to declare war on the United States, but not to an official declaration by the United States against China. The diplomacy and industrializing economy of the United States were thus linked with Latin America and Asia.

All of these situations created new constitutional tensions. Litigations from conquered provinces such as Puerto Rico and the Philippines, where McKinley (on his own authority) appointed military governors and civilian legislative commissions, questioned whether the Constitution followed the flag, that is, whether constitutional rights would be guaranteed to the inhabitants of U.S. territories. In the *Insular* cases (1901-11), the Supreme Court decided that if Congress incorporated a possession as American territory (not necessarily with future statehood in mind), then its residents enjoyed the Constitution's protections; residents of unincorporated possessions, however, did not. This formula sanctioned as much inequality for territory residents as the Court's separate-but-equal ruling in *Plessy v. Ferguson* (1896) had for southern blacks.

Ironically, the Court's judgments, so respectful of congressional prerogatives, came when presidential initiatives in diplomacy were escalating to imperial levels. This escalation resulted partially from Secretary of State John Hay's uses of executive agreements with foreign nations, which did not require congressional consent. Executive agreements (some secret) contrived by McKinley, Theodore Roosevelt, and Woodrow Wilson with Japan recognized the Japanese military protectorate over Korea and Japanese special interests in northern China. Russian and Japanese ambitions in Asia by 1905 resulted in a war between these two countries. Japan's shockingly overwhelming naval triumph so close to the Philippines left American policymakers unsure of the proper courses to take in that distant part of the globe.

Meanwhile, chronic political and economic instability afflicting Caribbean and Central American nations invited intervention by European powers. To thwart them, in 1895 then Secretary of State Olney expanded the Monroe Doctrine to assert an American right to protect Latin America's continuing independence from European domination. Ten years later, President Roosevelt announced his corollary to the Monroe Doctrine, one of prior right to intervene in an overindebted Latin American nation if economic or political instability tempted European powers to intervene. The Roosevelt Corollary converted the Monroe Doctrine from a vague attitude of the American government against further European colonization, one enforced less by American arms than by the self-interests and navy of the British, to a justification for vigorous intervention based on the increasing military power of the United States.

The Roosevelt Corollary spawned numerous interventions, which involved generations of American regulars in small-scale combats in the Caribbean and Central America during the next three decades, with the approval of Congress. American military and civilian provisional governments administered customs, tax, banking, transportation, medicine, school, and justice systems well into the 1930s. Whether writing constitutions for Haiti, establishing an honest customs service in the Dominican Republic, or training an antiguerrilla constabulary for Nicaragua, Americans (however well-intentioned) created enduring resentments that continue to shape the course of politics in the United States' sphere of influence.

Roosevelt mixed diplomacy and force in mediating the Russo-Japanese War, sending the American fleet around the world to show the flag, and in encouraging revolution in what became an independent Republic of Panama. In this last intervention, the United States won control over a zone in which it was able to build and run the Panama Canal but in which economic, racial, and legal biases added to anti-Yankee bitterness. All of this added fuel to the arguments of American anti-imperialists and legal experts who denied the president's unilateral capacity to order troops into foreign hazards, and created ponderous distinctions between "interpositions" (actions in which the commander-in-chief's only concern was the protection of American lives and property, a purpose not requiring congressional advice and consent) and "interventions" (short-of-war hostile actions toward the government of the affected country with intent to change that government, a purpose requiring congressional approval).

Prelude to World War I

When Democratic President Woodrow Wilson took office in 1913, he brought a new outlook to the presidency. A former university president and a vigorous Progressive reformer, Wilson had a high reputation as a constitutional scholar. Like his predecessors, Wilson unilaterally assigned regulars to hazardous foreign duties but chose also to seek congressional support as soon as possible after such assignments. He authorized the navy to bombard Vera Cruz and superficially to punish failures to salute the flag, but more basically, he intended to block German arms for anti-American Mexican factions. By joint resolutions Congress supported Wilson; international mediation defused the situation. In 1917, during a Mexican civil war, a faction led by Pancho Villa killed Americans in Mexico, New Mexico, and Texas. Wilson ordered the American army into Mexico with Senate (though not House) approval, at the nominal request of the Mexican president. When Villa evaded capture, American and Mexican troops savaged each other, yet both governments avoided a declared war. Wilson soon withdrew the American troops because of the priority of the European war that had begun in 1914.

Responding in 1916 to the German resumption of unrestricted submarine attacks on noncombatant shipping, Wilson requested authority from Congress to arm American merchantmen. When Congress refused, Wilson armed the merchantmen on his own authority. By early 1917 the drift toward a formal American war declaration against Germany became unmistakable. Officials worried that the 1867 *Milligan* decision would hamper effective policies.

Just before the American war declaration, Chief Justice White, in *Wilson v. New* (1917), sustained the 1916 Adamson Act provision for an eight-hour workday on railroads, asserting that in actual or impending emergencies the nation could do what in normal times it could not do. Crises did not create power, but they could call into play the Constitution's latent powers. White resurrected justifications for emergency constitutionalism from Lincoln's presidency, justifications the Court's *Milligan* majority had denied. The dissenting justices in *Wilson v. New* held fast to *Milligan,* asserting that the Constitution had no caves from which government, especially in peacetime, could suddenly emerge to diminish the assets of railroad companies by shortening workdays, particularly considering the due process clauses of the Fifth and Fourteenth Amendments.[6]

Peacetime was giving way to declared war even as the justices offered their views. It comforted Wilson that Lincoln and the pre-*Milligan* Supreme Court precedents allowed the *Wilson v. New* majority to modernize old emergency doctrines. Once at war, however, Wilson learned that the Court could only create doctrines, not implement them. During World War I Congress provided plenty of statutes for the exercise of martial power, and by delegating these statutory powers and using commander-in-chief authority, Wilson was able to fill in the gaps.

IV

Expanding War Powers, 1917-1940

Wilson shared with Progressives of both parties Lincolnian perceptions of a dynamic, adequate Constitution, of the inescapable accountability of officials, and of appropriate and timely ways to exert emergency powers. Commander-in-Chief Wilson, using both inherent executive powers and powers delegated by Congress in war-emergency laws, organized the labor forces and the economy in ways that affected civil liberties even more than during the Civil War. The accountability of officials became less important during the Wilson war years, reflecting the complex industrial and security needs of modern wars that necessitated serious curtailments of civil rights and liberties, rather than the threat of generals usurping civilian leaders' authority, which had been so prevalent in earlier conflicts.

This decrease in accountability resulted also because of a prewar Progressive innovation in public administration: the delegation of legislative authority to the president and subdelegations by him to both commissioned and unofficial subordinates.[1] The World War I Congress rarely specified agencies or officers to whom Wilson might subdelegate, and Wilson (or persons acting for him) sometimes subdelegated informally, even by telephone. At other times, Wilson accepted as implied delegations policies already initiated not only by national officials but also by state and local officials and by members of private or quasi-private groups.

Domestic Crises During and After World War I

The concerns of the neutrality years paved the way for this change. Between 1914 and 1917, while Europe waged a world war, the United States remained determinedly neutral, its regular army tiny enough to be contained in Yale's athletic stadium. Thin supplements existed in the form of volunteers and supporters of the military services, such as the Plattsburgh summer training camps, the National Security League, and the Navy League, all politically influential.

Meanwhile, reports circulated that German agents were sabotaging American industries, manipulating German and Irish "hyphenated-Americans" in the East, and corrupting migrant Wobblies in the West. (Supporters of the pacifist Industrial Workers of the World, Wobblies professed an anarchist creed, advocacy of which was a felony in several pro-employer Rocky Mountain and West Coast states.) In 1917 local police throughout the country were prejudiced against laborers and fearful of industrial spies. Federal criminal laws, including hangover Reconstruction statutes, related to neither spies nor industrial saboteurs. During a 1911 war scare with Japan, Congress had made the disclosure of military secrets a crime, but domestic industrial security remained a private business. Article of War No. 82 authorized army trials of spies caught on military property; neutrality laws (one dating from the 1790s) prohibited the enlistment of Americans to fight in foreign wars or hostile assaults on friendly nations. The 1878 Posse Comitatus Act restricted domestic uses of the army; an 1893 law forbade federal departments from hiring private detectives. But there were as yet no appropriate laws to deal with spies who threatened industries. In 1916 Wilson had appealed for more relevant criminal laws, but legislators had refused, fearing to favor the Justice Department's Bureau of Investigation (later FBI) over the Treasury's Secret Service, who were then feuding.[2]

Needing to act quickly after the declaration of war against Germany, Wilson did have a model of delegation to use, one that Congress had created in 1916 when it established a Council of National Defense (CND) to plan industrial and labor mobilization. Nominally directing the domestic war effort, Wilson delegated many of his own tasks to the CND, which in turn subdelegated, often to national, state, quasi-official, or wholly private entities. Accountability diminished, and complexities grew in administering basic policies. In the 1917 Lever Act, for example, Congress declared the entire food and fuel industries necessary for defense and delegated authority to Wilson to fix prices and set priorities. He assigned this work to the CND, which subdelegated to numerous state and local councils, a pattern advocated in many emergency statutes. When confusions multiplied, Wilson established on his own authority a War Industries Board and a Committee of Public Information to coordinate patriotic obedience to CND rules by industry and agriculture, management and labor. Largely staffed by volunteers, these agencies applied the nation's coercive war powers to the public by means of the president's delegations.

In 1917 General John J. Pershing, the head of the United States' forces, feared that he would require a million soldiers for homefront security duties against pro-German and Wobbly activists, an assignment likely to guarantee German victory. In response, two young government lawyers (in the president's name) simultaneously developed civilian analogs to the volunteer CND locals, the Navy and National Security leagues, and the Plattsburgh camps. Felix Frankfurter, then law asistant to the secretary of war, created the Loyal Legion of Loggers and Lumbermen (4Ls) as a civilian auxiliary to the army, and Walter Lippman, then assistant to the attorney general, launched the American Protective League (APL) as an auxiliary to the Department of Justice.

APL volunteers quickly formed local chapters in over two thousand communities nationwide. They assembled evidence for Espionage and Sedition Act prosecutions, especially those involving pro-German, anti-draft, and censorship violation allegations. In addition, the APL enforced food and fuel rationing, vice and liquor controls, bond-sale quotas, and liquor prohibitions, and helped to run conscription. Uncommissioned, unpaid, and ultimately undisciplinable, APL members were recruited primarily from among draft-exempt businessmen and professionals. They often equated class, racial, and religious biases with patriotism. Frequently in concert with local police or prosecutors, League members harassed antiwar publishers, conscientious objectors, radicals, labor union organizers, and racial equality advocates. After the November 1918 armistice, Justice officials withdrew government affiliation from the APL. Former League members contributed to postwar Red Scare excesses. Accountability was impossible in the essentially localist APL.

By contrast, the government continued to control the 4Ls, which embraced one war-essential northwestern industry, lumbering. In this industry Frankfurter saw the Wobblies less as a threat than as a problem resulting from owner refusals to improve workplaces and to deal with labor unions. Frankfurter and inventive army veterans of the Philippine military government created a Spruce Production Division (SPD) in the army, consisting of five thousand drafted woodsmen, an economical number compared to the million of Pershing's nightmare. The 4Ls was then organized as the SPD's civilian "voluntary" auxiliary. Legion locals recruited owner-operators and timberworkers, including Wobblies, to raise camp and mill conditions for workers to a level enjoyed by army privates. Profitable contracts and stable workforces pleased owners. APL and military intelligence agents exposed a few dissident workers, some of whom were drafted into the SPD. With little labor unrest to quell, the SPD cut timber alongside Legion members, and output soared. By early 1918 Legion cooperation between government, employers, and workers inspired imitations in Canada and talk of a permanent 4Ls in the United States, but after the armistice the army cut ties to the 4Ls, and employers refashioned local branches into company unions. Beginning with the 1919 Seattle general strike, industrial violence returned to the Northwest.

This unrest fed fears of Bolshevik uprisings nationwide. Local and state police and Bureau of Investigation agents, sometimes employing ex-League members, conducted "Red raids," deportation arrests, and political surveillances. The army prepared contingency plans for domestic uprisings.[3] Congress, however, exhibiting a laissez-faire, states' rights mood, repealed numerous economic and delegation statutes and abolished agencies born of subdelegations. Lawmakers overlooked other statutes, some of which would serve presidents as late as the 1970s.[4] The majority in

Congress agreed that the president retained independent authority to intervene militarily in strikes and race riots in Washington, D.C. and in the states, on appeals from governors.

In foreign affairs, the nation temporarily disfavored formal international commitments. The Senate refused to ratify the League of Nations treaty, which called for collective military responses against aggressors. Disarmament and abrogation-of-war treaties that the Senate did ratify seemingly diminished presidential capacities for independent diplomacy, yet in the 1918-32 years, the Senate exempted American "rights" under the Monroe Doctrine; sustained Wilson's commitment of fifteen thousand soldiers to an inter-Allied armed intervention against the new Soviet government; and approved, if only with money appropriations, the assignment of troops in numerous interventions, especially in the Caribbean, Central America, and China.

During this period the Supreme Court sustained World War I commander-in-chief, emergency, war, and treaty powers, including all legislative delegations to the president and presidential subdelegations, whether statutory or not. A common element in these decisions was their emergency context. In *Schenck v. U.S.* (1919), Justice Oliver Wendell Holmes, speaking for the unanimous Court, upheld the Espionage Act's censorship clauses and general purposes. Schenck's antidraft leaflets were a "clear and present danger"[5] to the warring nation and unprotected by the First Amendment. Congress therefore had a duty to anticipate and frustrate such dangers. The Court repeated the essence of this view in other 1919-20 decisions, including those in the *Frohwerk, Debs, Abrams,* and *Pierce* cases.[6] Furthermore, in *Missouri v. Holland* (1920), the Court suggested that a treaty protecting migratory fowl increased the Constitution's enumerated powers, even at the expense of state police powers, by embracing goals implicit in general welfare.

A generation thus schooled reasonably expected similar supports from both the Court and Congress when the Great Depression presented analogs for war. Veterans of World War I public service dominated the New Deal (Franklin Delano Roosevelt had been Wilson's assistant secretary of the navy). These veterans and so-called legal realists sought to adapt constitutionalism to crisis. In his March 1933 inaugural address, FDR asked Congress to delegate him power akin to that employable against a wartime invader. To rescue collapsing private banks, he used a holdover World War I trade-control law that Congress had forgotten to repeal, proclaiming the existence of a limited emergency, during which banks nationwide were required to close briefly because of a panic outflow of capital. In effect, FDR reversed the Wilsonian model of using a peacetime law during war and instead used a wartime law in a peacetime emergency.

In the Agricultural Adjustment Act (AAA) and the National Industrial

Recovery Act (NIRA), Congress delegated extensive authority to the president to aid farming and industry. Both the AAA and the NIRA rested on the commerce and tax powers and, as was true of all early New Deal statutes, on wartime-like crisis power. Congress skirted constitutional points while crafting the AAA, but stressed the Constitution during the NIRA's progress. NIRA champion Senator Robert Wagner, acknowledging that no declaration of emergency could increase the nation's powers, insisted that crisis enhanced what the Constitution allowed, an argument from *Wilson v. New*. Most Republicans, including important lawyers and academics, argued that *Ex parte Milligan* governed in peace and in crisis and that to accept the analogy between war and the Depression was to admit that the Constitution allowed self-preservation only by constitutional abandonment.

The first Supreme Court test of these positions involved a state rather than the nation. A Minnesota law postponed farm foreclosures, and claims of contract violations arose. In the *Blaisdell* decision (1934), Chief Justice Charles Evans Hughes, for a bare majority of the Court, sustained the state on *Wilson v. New* bases. In emergencies, a state's police powers could temporarily impede even contract enforcements, as in World War I rent controls. Perhaps an equivalent to war powers, beyond police power, existed for states. On the federal level, were the commerce and tax powers other equivalents?

Uncertain government lawyers soft-pedaled the war analogy in their briefs for the *Panama Refining* litigation (1935), which involved NIRA supports for state restrictions on oil production imposed to stop price drops, supports the justices condemned as excessive delegations of legislative power to the president. They reiterated this position in the *Schechter* (1935) and *Butler* (1936) decisions, in which Hughes (who now preferred *Milligan* to his own recent *Blaisdell* doctrine) condemned both the NIRA and the AAA. Deemphasizing *Wilson v. New* and *Blaisdell,* the Court decided that Congress, under the guise of emergency, had let delegation run riot; had harmed separation of powers; was regulating rather than encouraging commerce; and was not taxing for the general welfare. Furthermore, the Court ruled that the NIRA and the AAA eroded federalism.

By the end of 1936 emergency-power doctrine likened to war powers seemed dead, but the economic crisis remained. A Court majority less intransigent about restricting domestic emergency policies might have harmonized the NIRA and the AAA with *Wilson v. New* and *Blaisdell.* The jurists' extreme position, together with the 1936 reelection landslide, prompted Roosevelt's decision to "pack" the Court with younger appointees of presumably less rigid views. Congress rejected this bill, but enough of the justices learned moderation from the proposed legislation to sustain for forty years whatever uses Congress ordained for the tax and commerce power.

Perhaps the justices' maneuver of 1937 preserved the Court's capacity to raise sensitivity to the growth of the imperial presidency. Nevertheless, there is a Pyrrhic quality to the Court's victory of 1937, even if measured from foreknowledge of the judiciary's emergence in the 1950s and 1960s as the primary defender of individual civil rights and civil liberties. That emergence had begun in the *Gitlow* decision (1925), when the justices had asserted almost offhandedly that the First Amendment restrained states through the Fourteenth Amendment.[7] Civil libertarians were delighted with *Gitlow* because First and Fourteenth Amendment freedoms suffered far more at the hands of states and localities than at those of the nation. For a dozen years after *Gitlow,* however, the Court protected economic liberties overwhelmingly, culminating in *Schechter* and *Butler.* Having in those decisions rejected peacetime emergency economic powers and marked time on *Gitlow* implications, the justices accepted the broadest applications of the commerce, tax, and treaty powers in post-1937 decisions. Thus, when in December 1941 Japan catapulted the United States into a second world war, the Court was denying itself any significant governing roles at all.[8]

Prelude to World War II

Eroded by Italy's conquest of Ethiopia, Japan's inroads into China and Indochina, and Spain's civil war, the postwar treaty and disarmament systems collapsed, and World War II began in September 1939. FDR at first proclaimed U.S. neutrality, but later declared a limited national emergency, echoing the policies of the banking crises of 1933. This allowed him to select from the vast collection of hangover World War I statutes as unforeseen needs arose. He reestablished the statutory CND and an Office of Emergency Management on his own authority, while Congress enacted rearmament laws and created the United States' first peacetime draft.

These defense measures were overshadowed by Nazi Germany's total defeat of France, the Low Countries, and most of Scandinavia by mid-1940. Only Great Britain and the Soviet Union defied Hitler's domination in Europe; only a weak China resisted Japan in Asia. A potential linkage of totalitarian powers threatened the United States, yet isolationist sentiment remained strong and the armed forces relatively weak. In the House, only a single vote in 1941 extended the length of military service for new draftees. FDR nevertheless became willing to ignore neutrality as Britain, besieged by submarines and bombers, teetered toward collapse.

Soon after the fall of France in 1940, FDR expanded the Monroe Doctrine to deny the Nazis control of French, Dutch, and British colonies in the Americas. Executive agreements with the home governments-in-exile established American air and marine bases in Greenland and Iceland. FDR assigned the navy to a neutrality patrol around the Americas and then to convoys for Britain and later for Russia. The commanders of these convoys had orders to shoot at threatening subs and planes on sight. Convoy-hunting German patrol planes sometimes engaged these American forces in firefights, which were seldom reported in domestic media.

Though he did not consult Congress in advance on these matters, FDR did report fully to the legislators on the progress of these initiatives. He also pushed for collective enforcement of the Monroe Doctrine by all American nations, rather than by the United States unilaterally. The 1939 Declaration of Panama affirmed executive agreements to this effect with nineteen Latin American nations.

Changing foreign power relationships also deeply affected domestic policies. In 1940 FDR proclaimed the existence of an unlimited national emergency. Now he could, and did, call military reserves to active duty, regulate banking and foreign exchange, and govern industries he decided were essential to the nation's safety, including munitions, power, transportation, and communications. Roosevelt used these vast authorities rarely and restrainedly. A violent June 1941 strike in aviation plants resisted mediation and threatened warplane production. FDR, long identified as a close friend of organized labor, nevertheless nominally took over the facility, ordered troops to aid police in restoring order, and forbade picketing. Violence ceased, there were few arrests, and detentions were brief. Mediation ended the strike, and the troops withdrew. Similar interventions occurred in only two other instances, one involving shipbuilding and the other, aircraft instruments.[9]

While the Supreme Court all but hamstrung the president and Congress in domestic crises, it helped to keep foreign policymaking unfettered. In *Curtiss v. Wright* (1936), the Court virtually sanctioned boundless initiatives in the presidency when it denied that Congress's 1934 joint resolution, which delegated to the president discretion to embargo arms sales to warring Latin American nations, violated the Constitution. Justice George Sutherland asserted that in diplomacy the nation's executive authority predated the Constitution and that Congress could supplement inherent presidential discretion by delegating its authority. In the *Belmont* decision (1937), the Court blessed executive agreements.

In August 1940 FDR announced executive agreements for the American navy to patrol Canada's oceanic borders and for desperate Britain to receive fifty mothballed World War I destroyers in exchange for vital Caribbean bases. Legal experts convinced FDR that laws of 1883 and 1940 that restricted the discarding of warships useful for the American navy did not apply, and that *Curtiss* and *Belmont* controlled. At every step FDR conducted informal advise-and-consent consultations with congressional leaders, thereby respecting the essence of the Constitution. As with

Lincoln's aid to anti-secessionists in Virginia and Missouri after Sumter, FDR's destroyer-base deal was a timely constitutional response to the crisis.

After FDR's 1940 reelection, attention fastened on the Lend Lease Bill. Finally enacted in March 1941, this unprecedented statute, though not a war declaration, aligned the United States openly against the totalitarian conquerors of Europe. This law delegated authority to the president to sell, lease, or lend military materials to nations whose defense was deemed essential to the United States, as well as broad discretionary power to regulate the armaments industry. Although a clause allowed lawmakers to regain delegated powers by concurrent resolutions requiring only a simple majority, the passage of Lend Lease, after fierce and extended debate, ratified FDR's brinkmanship foreign policies. Thereafter, Roosevelt insisted that his pro-Allied policies implemented the Lend Lease Act rather than independent executive authority.

Eminent scholars concluded that FDR was less than candid because he presented Congress and the public with numerous *faits accomplis* in his uses of emergency power, especially in foreign policies, and that only the Japanese attack at Pearl Harbor saved him from constitutional crisis. Equally eminent holders of alternative views insisted that the evidence failed to confirm the duplicity argument and that every step in those fateful years was subject to the most intense public scrutiny.

Roosevelt took lessons from history with him in these steps. Labor-management conflicts, such as those in the aviation industry, generated no new proposals for leagues similar to the 4Ls. In internal security, FDR himself insured against any new APL or other arming of local prejudices with the government's war powers. In 1940 he won the assent of state governors for a total federal monopoly in internal security in the case of war. Accountability was the key to the argument. This concern over protection for civil liberties as a war approached gave the primary responsibility for domestic security to the FBI, a police institution that at least was part of a responsible government.[10] These policies would soon be tested, as the Japanese attack on Hawaii in December 1941 catapulted the United States into World War II.

V

Challenging War Powers, 1940-1960

World War II affected the United States in many complex ways. Wartime President Roosevelt exceeded Wilson and rivaled Lincoln in the use of war powers, a reflection of the clear and present dangers facing the United States in late 1941 (as in 1861, and more than in 1917). Fascist governments dominated Europe, North Africa, Japan, and much of China and Southeast Asia, and threatened India, Australia, and North Africa. In response to the Pearl Harbor attack, FDR successfully exploited Lockean-Lincolnian ideas about the legitimacy of crisis powers in a declared war and real crisis. Emergency doctrines for use in both foreign and domestic affairs were available, from the *Wilson v. New* and *Curtiss v. Wright* decisions, to hangover crisis statutes such as the 1917-18 Espionage-Sedition Act (rarely implemented in World War II), to FDR's own emergency declarations in 1939 and 1940. Yet FDR remained a party leader in a society in which constitutionalism, federalism, and two-party politics retained vitality as in no other warring nation.

World War II

Like Wilson, FDR preferred the comfort of statutes. Few members of Congress carped at his requests for laws delegating to him unlimited discretionary management of the nation's material and labor resources. On the bases of these delegations, hangover laws, independent executive war powers, and legal doctrines, FDR created implementing agencies, including those on emergency management, price administration, and war information. He even claimed a power to nullify one statute's provision for farm parity payments, dismissing it as contrary to sound wartime financing. Lawmakers, reluctant to force a constitutional confrontation, withdrew the provision. Similarly, few individuals irritated by abrasive war agencies transformed anger into constitutional litigation. Thus, although most war agencies could only advise, they were able to coerce effectively.

In 1943 and 1944, for example, coal miners and railroad workers held strikes without government interference, until war production suffered. FDR then ordered officials to operate the facilities until arbitration succeeded. Montgomery Ward's management refused, however, to re-contract with unions, despite War Labor Board rulings. Roosevelt ordered the secretary of commerce to operate Ward facilities until the company executives cooperated.

When the Supreme Court, in the *Steuart* decision (1944), refused to condemn as punitive seemingly arbitrary government oil rationing rulings, the president's economic war policies had the highest seal of constitutionality. Both the press and radio accepted voluntary restrictions so accommodatingly that the government almost never used emergency war powers against the media, a record perhaps unequaled globally. The postmaster general did bar from the mails publications of the rabidly anti-British, anti-Semitic priest, Father Charles Coughlin, under the Espionage Act. No litigation resulted from this action.

Regarding national security, officials remained relatively unconcerned about the millions of Americans of German and Italian extraction. State governors honored their 1940 commitment against local or amateur counterspying, and a seemingly professional federal monopoly existed in antidisloyalty operations. There *were* dangerous spies to catch.

Early in 1942 a German submarine landed eight Nazi soldier-spies near New York City, who planned to sabotage vital war industry. Captured and tried by a military court, they appealed for habeas corpus, as Merryman, Vallandigham, and Milligan had done eighty years earlier. The Supreme Court's unanimous *Ex parte Quirin* decision (1942) held that the military had tried the prisoners properly under both the international laws of war and the Fifteenth Article of War. Chief Justice Harlan Stone noted that both the president and Congress possessed war powers adequate to create military courts, and that if the Bill of Rights did not shelter American soldiers, then enemies were not entitled to constitutional protections.[1] In the *Cramer* treason case (1945), the government charged that a naturalized citizen had fed information to the saboteurs, an act witnessed by FBI agents. A five-justice majority was not convinced that this was overt aid to an enemy, as the Constitution required for a treason conviction. By contrast, the father of Herbert Haupt was found guilty of treason in 1947 for housing his son, who was one of the saboteurs, and recommending him for employment in a factory that made secret bombsights.

In the *Schneiderman* (1943) and *Baumgartner* (1944) decisions, the Supreme Court reversed naturalization proceedings that would have revoked the citizenship of a man who had concealed his Communist party membership and of another who was a vigorous Nazi sympathizer, holding that evidence of evil intent was not clear enough to warrant denaturalization. The Court applied this tight formula again in the *Hartzell* case (1944). Hartzell had written pro-Nazi pamphlets and distributed them to soldiers. The justices decided that the government had not proved intent to violate the 1917 Sedition Act's prohibition against undermining morale.

These World War II spy and treason cases did not trigger anti-German hysteria like that of 1917-19. Commissioned spycatchers and established military and civilian judicial procedures seemingly achieved both adequate security and acceptable justice. While protecting a few individuals, these procedures failed when, as in World War I, arbitrary categories of supposed mass disloyalty prevailed.

Hundreds of thousands of Japanese-Americans, both citizens and aliens, resided in California, Oregon, Washington, and Hawaii. FBI and army-navy intelligence failed to connect the Japanese-Americans to espionage or sabotage, but after Pearl Harbor contrary rumors fed on the traditional anti-Asian racism of the West Coast. Generals and governors transmitted racially prejudiced rumors to Washington. Hurried decision making in the federal government resulted in mass curfews, warrantless arrests, enforced relocations, and indefinite internments of over 120,000 Japanese, most of whom were American citizens, in detention centers under martial law.

Do mitigations exist for this racially discriminatory and arbitrary detention policy? Long discounted as mere masks for prejudice and greed, American military leaders' fear of actual invasions of Hawaii and the West Coast by the imperial Japanese seem now to have been more exaggerated than foolish or sinister, when weighed in the context of the stunning Japanese-Nazi successes in the Pacific, Europe, and the Middle East. John Stephan's *Hawaii Under the Rising Sun* (1984) suggests that Japanese planners had seriously considered invasion and intended to enlist Japanese in the United States in these operations. Despite such apprehensions, and their probable underlying racial prejudices, American authorities conducted the relocations without killing or wounding internees, in striking contrast to racially defined security analogs prevailing in Europe and Asia. By 1943 a statutory civilian agengy, the War Relocation Authority, replaced the military as camp administrators. Japanese-Americans cleared by FBI investigations were able to establish themselves in inland states, thereby permanently ending prewar ghettoes. Japanese-American volunteers formed the most decorated American combat regiment in Europe and performed peculiarly hazardous duties in the Pacific. Still, it cannot be discounted that an entire class of peacable Americans suffered severely as a result of the relocations.

In deciding the *Hirabayashi* appeal (1943), the Supreme Court unanimously sustained FDR's executive order of February 1942, which had authorized military officers to bar Japanese-Americans from controlled-access zones. As a result of this decision, some bitter internees chose future repatriation to Japan. In 1944 a majority of the justices in the *Korematsu* decision sustained the army's orders excluding Japanese from West Coast areas as a military necessity, but Justice Owen Roberts castigated the majority's refusal to consider the racial base of the linked exclusion-segregation-relocation policies.[2] FDR partially replaced military government in Hawaii with civilian authorities in 1944, and in *Duncan v. Kahanamoku* (1946), the Supreme Court decided that military trials of Hawaiian civilians were illegal after the president had restored habeas corpus in 1944.

The Cold War

Since 1945 endless undeclared international and civil wars, especially in Latin America, Vietnam, and the Mediterranean and Middle East regions, have frustrated U.S. foreign policies and strained domestic political and constitutional relationships. Strong presidents, assertive members of Congress, and occasionally rigorous justices (as well as academic analysts) have contested the nature of the war powers and the means to achieve internal security and changing foreign policy goals.

Between 1945 and 1960 public attention fixed on allegations that Soviet successes were explicable only because the Russians had so many supporters in public offices in the United States. President Harry Truman's 1947 executive order, which initiated loyalty tests for federal employees, opened this Pandora's box. Congress kept it open longer than was prudent for national self-interest, especially by means of investigating committees, and court judgments did not come down forthrightly on the sides of government duty or individual liberty.

The legislature's power to investigate is essential to responsible government. Some investigating committees during the cold war became harsh, allowing ruthless lawmakers armed with subpoenas, the power to punish for contempt, and immunity from lawsuit to harass individuals and groups. Red-hunting committees, such as the House Committee on Un-American Activities and the Senate Committees on Internal Security and Government Operation, fell under the control of demagogic partisans. Wisconsin Senator Joseph McCarthy, for example, helped to prostitute the investigative power into what Stanley Kutler called an "American Inquisition."[3] These tactics proved all the more dangerous after 1945 when the wartime agreement on a federal monopoly in security matters became obsolete, and several state legislative committees aped the McCarthy model.

Between 1945 and 1950 Congress terminated numerous wartime executive orders and statutes, yet left over one hundred either in force or dormant, as cold war tensions grew abroad. Congress was able to impose many qualifications on America's growing number of nonmilitary economic assistance programs, which required not only huge money appropriations by the House but also Senate confirmation of high-level appointees. Direct military programs proved to be far more difficult for Congress to control.

In 1947 Truman sent military relief supplies to "contain" a Marxist threat in Greece by encouraging local resistance. Subsequently enlarged as the Truman Doctrine, containment became a commitment against further Soviet domination anywhere in Europe and, finally, almost anywhere on the globe. Truman and Congress formalized the doctrine through executive agreements, statutes, and treaties, as in the Marshall Plan and the North Atlantic Treaty Organization (NATO). Cooperation between the White House and Capitol Hill reached new heights when in 1950 the Soviet Union imposed a total goods blockade on Berlin. Truman responded with a dramatic and risky paramilitary airlift of basic supplies to feed and fuel a major city. He asserted authority as commander-in-chief and under treaty obligations. Congress enthusiastically appropriated funds for the costly project. After a year, Russia lifted the blockade. Bloodless, successful, technologically exciting, and visible on television, containment seemed to work in Europe, as did crisis decision making in the United States.

Truman assumed that containment would also work in Asia, where in China a communist government had won a long civil war and was aiding sympathizers in North Korea. Without consulting Congress, Truman ordered American military forces to aid South Korea's infant government against invasion by communist North Korean troops in mid-1950. He claimed to have acted on the basis of a U.N. Security Council resolution that favored assistance to South Korea by member-states and triggered American treaty responsibilities. Truman also stressed his independent power as commander-in-chief to send troops into this undeclared war. It was no war, he insisted, even after China committed divisions of "volunteers" to assist the reeling North Koreans. It was a "police action," akin to numerous trivial expeditions against pirates or border raiders familiar to Americans since the 1790s. No one in 1950 could have foreseen the magnitude (55,000 American casualties), length (three years), and results (a divided Korea to the present) of the Korean combat. Truman, who added a new proclamation of emergency to those of 1939 and 1940 that were still in force, substantially advanced presidential discretionary prerogatives from old-fashioned gunboat diplomacy to major war making.

Congress supported Truman's Korean policy with money appropriations, but many congressional leaders were distressed at what seemed to be their slack reins over the White House. Truman's dismissal of General Douglas MacArthur from Korean command for insisting on military rather than civilian policy goals vindicated civilian control over the military, but it nevertheless helped to divide Congress further on liberal-conservative as well as party lines. A great debate took place over presidential war-making powers, the Bricker Amendment proposal, domestic security risks, and the 1950 Internal Security Act with its provisions (never implemented) for camps for political dissidents. (This debate would continue into Dwight D. Eisenhower's presidency, especially when in 1958 he ignored earlier congressional resolutions and ordered almost 15,000 American troops briefly into Lebanon.) It appeared that Congress had come close to losing all but reactive influences over war and security policies.

In 1952 Truman, applying his elastic views of a commander-in-chief's emergency powers in foreign affairs to the domestic scene, brought war powers into court. Desperate to prevent a threatened nationwide steelworkers' strike and lacking instructions from Congress despite his repeated requests, the president ordered the secretary of commerce to operate the vital properties. Industry management secured a temporary injunction against the secretary from a lower federal court; an appeal judge stayed the restraining order. In the *Youngstown* case (1952), the issues ascended to the Supreme Court.[4]

Youngstown, like *Dred Scott,* became a reservoir of frequently discordant opinions on basic questions. Only three dissenting justices sustained Truman's actions as consistent with the pattern of retrospective congressional supports for executive anticipatory initiatives in crises, extending back at least to Lincoln and relying heavily on the Article II "take care" clause. Six justices held, however, that Truman's order confused necessary presidential initiatives on foreign affairs with an unconstitutional usurpation of Congress's now traditional powers to regulate the internal economy. Statutory procedures existed for preventing damaging strikes. Truman had acted outside those procedures.

In an earlier case, *Woods v. Miller* (1948), Justice Robert Jackson had worried about the vague, undefined, and undefinable war powers. The Framers had understood emergencies, but except for the habeas corpus suspension provision in the Constitution, they had preferred procedures to arbitrary actions. "We may also suspect," Jackson noted, "that they suspected that emergency powers would tend to kindle emergencies." Jackson compared war-emergency habits in several foreign nations to those in the United States; this convinced him that no American president should wield emergency powers unless external sentries in Congress and, less commonly, in the Supreme Court, checked excesses. Congress had chosen, without statute, to delegate anticipatory emergency powers in such situations as a steel strike to the executive, but these powers were to remain dormant until need arose. "Under this [familiar] procedure we retain Government by law—special, temporary law, perhaps, but law nonetheless." Without statute, executive crisis power "... either has no beginning or it has no end. If it exists, it need submit to no legal restraint. I am not alarmed that it would plunge us straightway into dictatorship but it is at least a step in that wrong direction."[5] Congress, not the Court, must be the primary obstacle to executive prerogatives, Jackson concluded.

Jackson has been proven correct. In his words, a dangerous "zone of twilight" on the war powers remains in the Constitution, because "any actual test of power is likely to depend on the imperatives of events and contemporary imponderables rather than on abstract theories of law."[6] But abstract theories of law have been weak reeds to use as staffs in defining the war powers. When the Supreme Court and Congress have searched for ways to enforce accountability on at least some presidents, they have resorted to overly neat legal and constitutional abstractions. For example, in 1804 Chief Justice John Marshall, in *Little v. Barreme,* established the principle that unless a president's actions were essentially political—and the question of whether an action is political, and thus not subject to judicial decision, is itself troublesome—presidential military subordinates would be held strictly accountable for their acts, even though carried out under orders. This principle was forcefully restated six decades later by influential law writer Thomas McIntyre Cooley in books that were to be standard texts in law schools until well after World War I. Events of the 1960s to the present would exhibit how unfixed the principle of Marshall and Cooley was, and how acute were Justice Jackson's apprehensions about the relevance of the Constitution to the war powers and to the stability of American society.

VI

Redefining War Powers, 1960-1985

Constitutional historian Herman Belz estimated that a primary danger for constitutional government was the presidentially proclaimed state of emergency. If such executive proclamations "... became a permanent affair the constitutional barriers upon the scope of peacetime federal power and upon the executive power in time might crumble away."[1] Other dangers exist. Some major successes, as well as many stalemates and reverses, have marked American diplomacy ever since the cold war began to chill hopes for peaceful international relationships and required the maintenance of relatively large armed forces in peacetime. Observers have worried about the means of keeping military and intelligence services constitutionally accountable, especially since they have become rivals for missions and appropriations.

Even more difficult is the problem of achieving the accountability of the civilian covert intelligence agencies that have developed since 1945. This proliferation has created an American intelligence community that has not only collected data but has also conducted warlike, covert, paramilitary, and guerrilla operations against governments deemed unfriendly and, more recently, has searched for ways effectively to combat terrorists acting for both governments and private groups. Critics of these agencies insist that the actions of the intelligence community have imperiled the constitutional vessel, if only because accountability is so uncertain. Their defenders insist that such covert operations in a predatory world of overlapping, undeclared, warlike crises are as essential as the broad discretions that navy officers received to punish Barbary pirates in Jefferson's time. Many insist that adequate accountability does exist, as even the Central Intelligence Agency (CIA) is considering opening some of its files to lawmakers and scholars.

The Creation of the CIA

In the 1947 National Security Act, Congress created the CIA to succeed a World War II improvisation, the Office of Strategic Services. Lawmakers made the CIA responsible to the National Security Agency, which was to be overseen by the National Security Council composed of the secretary of defense, the director of the CIA, and the joint chiefs of staff. According to the statute, the president could not add to the National Security Council without prior Senate approval, but every president since Eisenhower has appointed an unauthorized National Security advisor, who was not subject to Senate confirmation. Although the office is still extralegal, its influential incumbents have evolved into the Security Council's chief administrators. Under this politically fluctuating leadership, the CIA took over the FBI's foreign operations, leaving the latter to concentrate on domestic security work.[2]

In the early 1950s Congress tried to enlarge CIA accountability, requiring the CIA to participate in annual hearings of all intelligence agencies covering Soviet developments. But the CIA covert operations that Eisenhower authorized, including those aimed at stabilizing Lebanon's ill-fated government and at destabilizing leftist governments in Guatemala and Cuba, suggest that this was a modest rein.

President John F. Kennedy was still moving into the White House in 1961 when Eisenhower told him of the impending CIA-sponsored attack at the Bay of Pigs by émigré Cubans against the Fidel Castro government. Kennedy chose not to cancel the expedition, which failed abysmally. A year later, on the basis of an accurate CIA report, Kennedy had the navy block Soviet missiles being shipped to Cuba, without formally consulting Congress. The resulting standoff risked nuclear war, but the USSR recalled the rockets. Most of Congress supported Kennedy's swift, unilateral action because the threats were real and immediate, conditions that future presidents would overlook.

Assuming office after Kennedy's assassination, President Lyndon B. Johnson quickly came to favor wide presidential discretion to define and defend against external threats. In 1965, ostensibly to protect American lives and property abroad when a host government failed to do so (but more probably to undercut seemingly pro-Marxist governments), Johnson sent large forces briefly to the Dominican Republic. More fatefully, he committed the United States to what would be its longest, most divisive war, in Vietnam (a part of former French Indochina), a war in which the immediacy of real danger to the United States never became clear.

The Vietnam War

Johnson, and presidents after him, misread war powers history. Lincoln's improvisations had been in the domestic context of the Civil War. McKinley's commitment of substantial forces to quell Filipino and Boxer rebels, Wilson's Siberian expedition, and FDR's assignment of marines to Iceland had never neared the duration, the massive numbers (eventually more than 500,000), the casualties, and the costs that Vietnam would demand. Truman had enjoyed U.N. and treaty sanctions for Korea. JFK had reacted to the visible dangers of Soviet missiles in nearby Cuba. LBJ himself had justified the Dominican Republic intervention on the basis of rescuing American civilians. But in 1964 only a handful of

Americans, principally military advisors, were in Vietnam to implement assistance programs approved earlier by Congress.

Politically, if not constitutionally, a strong sanction for enlarged American intervention in Vietnam was wise.[3] LBJ therefore won congressional approval in the Tonkin Gulf Resolution of August 1964, which addressed attacks that had allegedly occurred on American warships near North Vietnam. The resolution was passed unanimously by the House and nearly unanimously by the Senate. This resolution approved all necessary measures to be taken by the president to repel armed attacks against U.S. forces and to prevent further aggression.

Even basic facts about the Tonkin Gulf attack remain disputed. Allegations persist that details on the attack were ill-reported and possibly distorted, perhaps even by the president, to the point of misleading (if not deceiving) Congress and the public into accepting further intervention in Vietnam. If this were so, why did LBJ not exploit the consensus of mid-1965 and have Congress declare war? After 1965 Johnson was not again able to mobilize public support for the conflict.

In 1968 Johnson declined to seek reelection. Succeeding Johnson, President Richard Nixon widened the Vietnam War by ordering secret bombing raids of Cambodia, a shelter for hostile forces, even though Congress had stipulated in 1969 in a National Commitments Act that foreign policy commitments by the United States required both legislative and executive affirmative action. In addition, a joint resolution prohibited funds for expanding the war to Laos and Cambodia. In 1970 Nixon ordered large American land forces into Cambodia. Antiwar demonstrations at home became violent; the demonstration at Kent State University ended in deaths. Publication of highest-level policy documents such as *The Pentagon Papers* (1971), despite threats of prosecution by the Nixon administration under the 1917 Espionage Act, illuminated subterfuges aimed at justifying these uses of war powers. After bitter disagreements, Congress utilized the Cooper-Church rider to a military appropriations bill and denied funds to a president during a shooting war (the Cambodian intervention) for the first time in American history. Nixon saved face by proclaiming the expedition a success and withdrew the troops from Cambodia.

Congress could only prevent this particular use of the war powers by a painfully achieved budget tug; Congress could not yet force an end to the Vietnam conflict. More immediately, Congress repealed the Tonkin Gulf Resolution in December 1971 but did not specify that a war justified on that authority must end. Nixon, feeling himself still unfettered, in 1972 responded to North Vietnamese army assaults in South Vietnam with massive aerial bombings of the North. He viewed his landslide second-term election as a plebiscite both for his war policies and for the 1973 peace accord that ended American land involvement in Vietnam (Nixon maintained significant American air and naval activity until the North Vietnamese total victory in April 1975). Congress appeared to be a mere bystander in peacemaking as well as in war making, and the courts offered Nixon's critics few comforts.

In *New York Times v. U.S.* (1971), the Supreme Court rejected the government's argument that publication of *The Pentagon Papers* would harm the nation and violate the 1917 Espionage Act. A year later, the Court denied the president's inherent power to conduct warrantless domestic wire-tapping surveillances. But in 1967 the Court had twice refused to hear allegations of the unconstitutionality of American involvement in the Vietnam undeclared war and in 1970 had let stand a lower court ruling *(Massachusetts v. Laird)* that Congress, by appropriating funds, among other actions, had concurred in the president's orders. In 1973 the Supreme Court sustained a lower court's stay of an injunction that forbade the president from continuing the allegedly unconstitutional war, reaffirming, in *Holtzman v. Schlesinger,* the political-question doctrine and in effect leaving the war powers without judicial definition.[4]

Reassertion of Congressional War Powers

Although Congress was confused about the war powers, it continued to reassert a coequal authority to control those powers, especially as Vietnam and Watergate corroded Nixon's leadership, culminating in his resignation to avoid impeachment. Senate and House committees, the primary vehicles of this reassertion of congressional power in war-emergency matters, heard experts from government and academe. Unsurprisingly, witnesses who supported the Nixon administration argued that history had "proved" the hazards and unconstitutionality of limiting a commander-in-chief even in solo war making on a Vietnam scale, usually after recounting the total presidential independent martial commitments since 1789. Such champions insisted that war powers issues were always volatile, not static; that tensions between the government's branches must not be resolved by rigid procedures capable of inhibiting effective responses to crises; and that a president could exceed commander-in-chief powers only if egregiously abusing that vague authority. While agreeing on the Constitution's necessary adaptability, other respected constitutional scholars testified that adequate responses to past crises had occurred notwithstanding relatively scrupulous obedience to checks and balances; that secret budgets for undeclared wars and covert operations were dangerous to healthy constitutionalism; and that modern emergencies involved such basic and huge stakes that new efforts by Congress to implement the Constitution with more effective war powers procedures were justified.

Some analysts observed that Congress's party discipline was too diminished, its committee structure too decentralized, its statute-drafting and budgetary operations too numerous and unsynchronized, and its tugs from diverse constituencies too diffused for the effective checking of a strong president's war powers. Many representatives, reflecting their constituents' president-centeredness, especially in foreign affairs, were unwilling to tie Nixon's hands. But the bombings in Cambodia and Laos, and Watergate spinoffs, were creating a voting coalition in Congress that favored long-term rather than single procedural controls and a reassertion of congressional power to define a president's power to use the military defensively. Although proposals aimed at these ends died in the 1970-72 congressional sessions, in 1972 Congress did require the secretary of state to submit the texts of all executive agreements within sixty days after they took effect, thus at least opening possibilities that the House might twist purse strings or join the Senate in other nonimplementations.[5]

In 1973 Congress passed the War Powers Act. This measure established procedures for the president to follow when unilaterally ordering American troops to intervene in undeclared foreign combat situations. With the War Powers Act, Congress planned to force presidential accountability for short-of-declared war policies, primarily by forcing the president to report to Congress within sixty days of the assigning of troops to combat duty abroad; a violation would invite legislative vetoes of the commander-in-chief's orders. The act read the Constitution as giving Congress control of all combat commitments except defenses of U.S. territory from invasions. The act also blended elements suggested since 1971: in the absence of a war declaration, hostilities initiated by a president were to follow consultation with Congress, to be followed in turn by the president's reporting in writing to Congress within forty-eight hours of ordering troops into combat; this also would apply when hostilities were probable or when the number of troops already in a combat area had to be substantially increased. Congress exempted NATO and similar treaty commitments and the CIA from coverage and imposed a sixty-day limit on the action (Congress had the option to extend the sixty-day limit). Congress could impose its now popular legislative veto on unwelcome military policies in the form of a veto-proof concurrent resolution, which required majority votes in both houses but not a president's signature. If Congress were to issue such a veto, the president would have to remove troops from combat. Such vetoes might trigger the curtailment of supportive funds and other discretionary congressional controls over the executive and the military. In effect, both houses of Congress could now advise and consent.[6] In early October 1973 the bill passed both houses of Congress, and Nixon, like Andrew Johnson a century earlier, by a veto created a majority adequate to override.

Nixon contended that Congress could not constitutionally redefine presidential war powers practices. Exalting one function, the commander-in-chief's, and one government branch, the executive, above all others, Nixon equated Jefferson's minor expeditions against Barbary pirates and Lincoln's policies in a titanic domestic civil war with the distant, undeclared Vietnam War. Congress overrode Nixon's veto in November 1973.

The War Powers Act and Congress's related efforts were neither triumphs nor tragedies. The act was a significant bipartisan effort for the first time to balance the solo war-making initiatives of an imperial presidency with Congress's duty to declare war, and to add newer procedures relevant to nonmilitary or paramilitary entities like the CIA to traditional procedures aimed at civilian control over the military.

Among related efforts, Congress tried to increase accountability for CIA covert operations, despite the exemption of the CIA from coverage under the War Powers Act, but found the task of monitoring the CIA complex and difficult. The 1974 Hughes-Ryan Amendment to the 1961 Foreign Assistance Act forbade funds to the CIA for anything other than intelligence work, unless the president or the CIA director certified each substantive operation as necessary for national security by a timely report to the House and Senate Select Committees on Intelligence. In addition to disclosures about poor monitoring of CIA operations, in 1974 a Senate report found 470 provisions of federal statutes that could be triggered during a war or a national emergency by either the president or Congress. Many dealt with innocuous domestic topics, such as presenting medals to soldiers, low-interest loans to flooded areas, money relief to school systems affected by nearby military installations, and stockpiling foodstuffs for civil defense. Some legislators worried whether civil defense, for example, was properly a war power or a state's traditional police power. But the CIA, for a while at least, remained the primary concern of Congress and others who had become very sensitive to the enormous growth of war and emergency authorities.

Also in 1974 Congress created a congressional budget office to arm lawmakers with fiscal data equivalent to that available to the president. Each house of Congress established a budget committee to present resolutions on a budget, including military and intelligence programs. Amendments of 1974 and 1976 to the Foreign Military Sales Act required a president to notify Congress in advance of arms sales valued at $7 million (formerly $25 million) or more and to wait thirty days before delivering the arms. If the sale were an emergency national security need of the country, a president could, in effect, override Congress. Conversely, Congress could disapprove by concurrent resolution, initiating another thirty-day delay. As in all these laws, the procedures encouraged consultation and consensus while allowing adequate freedom of action in the White House in genuine crises.

Nixon's unwilling resignation brought Gerald R. Ford to the presidency. Ford initiated a bewildering succession of CIA directors, whose brief reigns left the agency's power buried in its obscure lower administration. Ford exhibited his own large views on executive initiatives and encountered Congress's recent self-assertiveness on war powers. Congress rejected his requests for large new military and CIA appropriations, which many in Congress regarded as implicit compliances with the War Powers Act, except to rescue Americans from South Vietnam and Cambodia.

When Cambodians captured the American merchant ship *Mayaguez,* Ford ordered navy-marine units to free the captive crew without consulting Congress, thereby failing to obey the War Powers Act; nevertheless, Congress applauded. Had Ford created a precedent for after-the-fact rather than prior consultation by a president with Congress as adequate to satisfy the War Powers Act, when Congress agreed with presidential aims and means? What would happen if Congress disagreed?[77]

These questions were answered to a certain extent when the CIA and agencies of Cuba, South Africa, the USSR, and the People's Republic of China supported contending factions in a grinding civil war in Angola. Ford, arguing that a failure to supply funds would lead to a Marxist victory, failed to convince Congress that this consequence directly threatened the United States.

Succeeding Ford, President James Earl Carter accentuated detente with the Soviet Union and discretionary support for human rights in Latin America, demonstrating in part a shifting of aid from cruelly repressive nations to others exhibiting democratic practices. In 1979, with Cuban aid, Nicaraguan Sandinista (the name refers to anti-U.S. activist Nicaraguans of the 1920s and 1930s) rebels overthrew that country's military tyrant. In the same year, in distant Iran, a revolutionary government's repressive theocracy trapped the United States in an ultimately humiliating hostage situation, one in which the climactic effort at military intervention was tragically inadequate. Thereafter, some governments increasingly embraced official terrorism as policy, adding to burdens on Americans already imposed by private terrorists. These developments limited (and continue to limit) the United States' capacities to respond, except perhaps by massive military power or by covert operations applied regionally, as in the nearby Caribbean but not in distant Vietnam, Lebanon, and Iran, or in peripatetic terrorist hijackings of commercial aircraft and cruise ships, with their numerous helpless passengers, in 1985.

These last developments further confused congressional efforts to recapture a larger role in war powers decisions. During the Iranian hostage crisis, for example, Congress generally agreed on the need for Carter's abortive military expedition and seemed to say that the rescue force was not governed by the War Powers Act. Indications were, and are, that Congress would test presidential compliance by the context of each crisis and then decide if and how to exert the ancient power of the purse or the recent law on war powers.

In 1981 President Ronald Reagan called for avoidance of direct confrontation with the USSR, while attempting to capitalize on the Soviet Union's own difficulties by increasing American military rearmament. Meanwhile, the United States, admitting its inability to affect the internal and borderland policies of the Soviet Union, encouraged the Soviets to pull the reins on their surrogate states such as Cuba. This revived spheres-of-influence policy continues to work itself out in the context of instability in Afghanistan, Lebanon, and Latin America.

Alleged Marxist guerrillas were destabilizing pro-U.S., if regrettably repressive, regimes in Honduras, Guatemala, and El Salvador. In 1981 Reagan increased the number of American military advisors in El Salvador. Congress asserted that this action came under the War Powers Act, and Reagan reluctantly promised not to increase their number or to hazard them in combat. Congress's triumph in a situation that involved less than three-score advisors was largely symbolic. American forces remained nearby, participating frequently in military-naval maneuvers with forces of friendly neighboring governments, often under a regional treaty. Covert CIA operations against Nicaragua continued.

In August 1982 Reagan sent two thousand marines to Lebanon as part of a multinational force to oversee the withdrawal of the Palestine Liberation Organization after its defeat by Israel. Although the marines suffered some minor casualties in Lebanon's civil war, Reagan insisted that they were not in a combat zone, yet he sometimes also admitted that the War Powers Act applied. In April 1983, in the Lebanon Emergency Assistance Act, Congress required prior statutory approval "for any substantial expansion"[8] of the American military mission. In October Reagan obtained a resolution extending the sixty-day limit (beginning from a date when several marine fatalities occurred) that the War Powers Act placed on troop presence in Lebanon's warlike situation to eighteen months. He also insisted that in signing the resolution he was not admitting that the War Powers Act bound him. Two weeks later, after a terrorist suicide bombing killed 250 marines, Reagan withdrew the detachment, still not admitting obedience to the War Powers statute.

Like his predecessors, Reagan opposed the growth of leftist governments in the Caribbean as well as in Latin America. In October 1983, without consulting Congress but after conferring with representatives of the Organization of Eastern Caribbean States (OECS), Reagan ordered a large-scale American invasion of the tiny island-nation, Grenada, assertedly to honor OECS fears about the leftist government and to protect American students in Grenada. The Grenadan government was unseated, and Reagan recalled the troops before the expiration of the sixty-day period of emergency presidential authority stipulated in the War Powers Act, leaving the question of its applicability hanging.

Presidents since Nixon have been little constrained by attempts to restrict executive war powers. After all, from 1973 to 1983 Congress left the War Powers Act substantially uninvoked. High courts in the last decade exhibited only occasional willingness to explore the twilight zone of executive power in undeclared foreign wars and to lessen exclusions justified by the political-question doctrine. In doing so, these courts largely sustained presidential positions, leading to Edward Keynes's conclusion: "Unless Congress exercises its constitutional authority to restrain executive power, opponents of constitutional dictatorship should not await a judicial David to slay an executive Goliath."[9]

A Retrospect

The Constitution institutionalized multiple voices in competition and tension in congressional, presidential, and judicial duties and structure. That structure has endured, however altered by changed catalogs of duties, in-house rules, and party realignments, for two centuries. No compelling reasons justify abandoning or even seriously modifying the Constitution. America's foreign problems are going to endure, and tinkering with the Constitution will not eradicate or solve these problems. The Constitution requires Congress to participate in the means that it, and presidents, evolve to cope with them. Intelligence agencies and covert operations appear to be as much parts of modern governments as are undeclared wars. But for Americans, the 1787 Constitution retains its character as the test by which the validity of means—including military and near-military means—as well as the ends of foreign policy are established.

Is it possible to stand between polar views and devise more precise formulas than those of the 1973 War Powers Act for responding constitutionally to private terrorism, near-wars, quasi wars, and terrorist wars of liberation, which are the lot of modern society? If the arduous nature of this labor is caused by the frequent failure of the Framers' creation to work tidily, nevertheless their wisdom is again manifest in their avoidance of overly precise definitions, which would now be obsolete. The Constitution's very ambiguities and structure encourage middle-range responses between inaction and nuclear strike. It does not follow that a president should make solo war or warlike decisions, except perhaps in the case of a nuclear attack. Instead, consultation at every step in an ascending crisis should always occur, thus allowing Congress to perform its constitutional duties by asserting its constitutional authority: the House on appropriations and the Senate on the power to advise and consent.

In 1985 Americans must once again go back to the 1787 Constitution, to Lincoln's fear of 1862 that the dogmas of a mythical quiet past might no longer serve a stormy present. To echo Lincoln once again, it is time to remember that in the crisis conditions that humankind has not found ways to evade, the Constitution's war powers remain "our main reliance."

NOTES

Preface

[1]3 January 1899, Special Collections Library, Columbia University.

Introduction

[1]*Messages and Papers of the Presidents,* ed. James D. Richardson (New York, 1901), VI: 142, 191.

[2]W. H. Auden, *Collected Poems,* ed. Edward Mendelson (London, 1976), 465.

[3]T. S. Eliot, *Four Quartets* (New York, 1943), 39.

Chapter I

[1]John Reid, *In a Defiant Stance* (University Park, Pa., 1977).

[2]Arthur Schlesinger, jr., *Imperial Presidency* (Boston, 1973), 14.

[3]Morris Greenspan, *The Modern Law of Land Warfare* (Berkeley, 1959), 35-39; J. F. C. Fuller, *The Conduct of War* (New Brunswick, N.J., 1961), 15-25.

[4]*Papers of Thomas Jefferson,* ed. Julian P. Boyd (Princeton, 1958), XV: 397.

[5]Richard Longaker, intro. to Clinton Rossiter, *The Supreme Court and the Commander in Chief* (Ithaca, 1976), 11-12.

[6]Ibid., 12.

[7]*U.S. Statutes at Large,* I: 570.

[8]George M. Dennison, "Martial Law: The Development of a Theory of Emergency Powers, 1776-1861," *American Journal of Legal History,* 18 (1974): 52; see also essays by A. H. Bowman on Jefferson and by Abbot Smith on Madison in *The President's War Powers,* ed. Demetrios Caraley (New York, 1984).

[9]Dwight F. Henderson, "Civil Liberties and the War of 1812," paper delivered at the third annual meeting of the Society for Historians of Early America, July 1981.

[10]Martin v. Mott, 12 Wheaton 19 (1827).

[11]Abraham D. Sofaer, *War, Foreign Affairs, and Constitutional Power: The Origins* (Cambridge, Mass., 1976).

Chapter II

[1]*Annals of Congress,* 14th Cong., 1st sess., March 1816, 1192.

[2]*The Collected Works of Abraham Lincoln,* ed. Roy P. Basler (New Brunswick, N.J., 1953), I: 451-52.

[3]Luther v. Borden, 7 Howard 1 (1849).

[4]See Harold M. Hyman and William M. Wiecek, *Equal Justice Under Law: Constitutional Development, 1835-1875* (New York, 1982), ch. 8.

[5]Peter Maslowski, *Treason Must Be Made Odious* (Millwood, N.Y., 1978).

[6]Lincoln knew that Taney wanted the Court to oppose military action and thereby render government operations impossible. Taney prepared decisions-without-cases, declaring wartime policies on conscription, emancipation, and Reconstruction unconstitutional, but government lawyers did not initiate suits that would involve such tender political questions. These questions were decided by the voters.

[7]*Messages and Papers,* ed. Richardson, VI: 22-23.

[8]*Collected Works of Lincoln,* ed. Basler, VII: 281-82.

[9]Ibid., VIII: 254-55.

Chapter III

[1]Ex parte Milligan, 4 Wallace 2 (1867).

[2]Donald G. Nieman, *To Set the Law in Motion* (Millwood, N.Y., 1979).

[3]Michael Les Benedict, *A Compromise of Principle* (Millwood, N.Y., 1974).

[4]C. Vann Woodward, *Reunion and Reaction* (Boston, 1951).

[5]*Revised Statutes,* ch. 2001, 15 *Statutes* 224 (27 July 1868).

[6]Michael R. Belknap, "The New Deal and the Emergency Powers Doctrine," *Texas Law Review,* 62 (1983): 79-80.

Chapter IV

[1]Nathan D. Grundstein, *Presidential Delegation of Authority in Wartime* (Pittsburgh, 1961).

[2]Harold M. Hyman, *To Try Men's Souls* (Berkeley, 1959), ch. XI; Joan M. Jensen, *The Price of Vigilance* (Chicago, 1968).

[3]Ibid.; see also "U.S. Military Intelligence Reports: Surveillance of Radicals in the United States, 1917-1941," microfilm (Frederick, Md., 1984). The army also lobbied Congress unsuccessfully for antilynching laws because black soldiers suffered unpunished assaults, especially in southern states. Claudine Ferrell, "Nightmare and Dream" (PhD diss., Rice University, 1983).

[4]See Reuben Clark, *Emergency Legislation* (Washington, 1918), and U.S. Senate, Special Committee on the Termination of the National Emergency, *Summary of Emergency Power Statutes* (Washington, 1973).

[5]Schenck v. U.S., 249 U.S. 47, 52 (1919).

[6]Paul Murphy, *World War I and the Origins of Civil Liberties in the United States* (New York, 1979), 183, chs. 2, 7.

[7]Klaus H. Heberle, "From *Gitlow* to *Near," Journal of Politics,* 34 (1972): 458.

[8]Paul Murphy, *The Constitution in Crisis Times* (New York, 1972), chs. 1-6; Belknap, "New Deal and Emergency Powers Doctrine," 67.

[9]Louis W. Koenig, *The Presidency and the Crisis* (New York, 1944), 12-13, 78; Harold Relyea, *Brief History of Emergency Powers in the United States,* 93d Cong., 2d sess., 32-40.

[10]Kenneth O'Reilly, "A New Deal for the FBI," *Journal of American History,* 69 (1982): 638.

Chapter V

[1]These views were reinforced by the *Yamashita* decision (1944), which denied protection under the Constitution to a captured enemy officer who had been convicted for violating the laws of war. See Richard L. Lael, *The Yamashita Precedent* (Wilmington, Del., 1982).

[2]Peter Irons, *Justice at War* (New York, 1983). In 1983 a federal judge in California threw out Korematsu's 1944 conviction and criminal record on the basis of proof (some drawn from FBI files) of official knowledge of Korematsu's innocence forty years earlier. The 1944 decision still controls, however, justifying a concern that future suffering might occur through unwarranted application of emergency doctrines to a race.

[3]Stanley I. Kutler, *The American Inquisition* (New York, 1982).

[4]See Maeva Marcus, *Truman and the Steel Seizure Case* (New York, 1977).

[5]Woods v. Miller, 333 U.S. 138, 141, 146 (1948).

[6]Youngstown Sheet and Tube Co. v. Sawyer, 343 U.S. 579 (1952).

Chapter VI

[1]Alfred Kelly, Winfred Harbison, and Herman Belz, *The American Constitution* (New York, 1983), 575; see also U. Alexis Johnson, *Right Hand of Power* (Englewood Cliffs, 1984).

[2]See Thomas F. Troy, *Donovan and the CIA* (Frederick, Md., 1981); Stansfield Turner, *Secrecy and Democracy: The CIA in Transition* (Boston, 1985); Anna K. Nelson, "President Truman and the Evolution of the National Security Council," *Journal of American History,* LXXII (1985): 360; Loch K. Johnson, *Season of Inquiry: The Senate Intelligence Investigation* (Lexington, Ky., 1985); and John M. Oseth, *Regulating U.S. Intelligence Operations: A Study in Definition of the National Interest* (Lexington, Ky., 1985).

[3]LBJ's supporters argued that the South East Asia Treaty bound the United States to defend Vietnam and that both the treaty and the Tonkin Gulf Resolution were self-executing; LBJ did not seem to be comfortable with this authority. Eugene V. Rostow, "Great Cases Make Bad Law," *Texas Law Review,* 50 (1972): 833.

[4]In 1984 the Supreme Court agreed to hear *CIA v. Sims,* in which the CIA had been required to release information on researchers whose evidence had resulted in certain covert

activities, but it is not certain that a decision would address basic war powers questions. In the same year the Reagan administration threatened to prosecute under the Espionage Act a former official who had disclosed confidential information.

[5]Harvey G. Zeidenstein, "The Vietnam War and the Reassertion of Congressional Power," in *President's War Powers,* ed. Caraley, 163-79.

[6]The Supreme Court disapproved the legislative veto in Immigration and Naturalization Service v. Chadha, 103 S.Ct. 2764, 2780-81 (1983).

[7]See House Subcommittee on International Security, *War Powers: A Test of Compliance,* 94th Cong., 1st sess., 1975.

[8]90 *Stat.* 762, 30 June 1976.

[9]Edward Keynes, *Undeclared War* (University Park, Pa., 1982), 160.

Suggestions For Further Reading

All of the United States' wars, whether declared or undeclared, foreign as in Vietnam or domestic as in the Civil War, as well as nonwar domestic crises including the Dorr Rebellion, Pullman strike, and Red Scares, generated extensive constitutional arguments. A vast literature is available on the war-initiating, war-executing, and war-ending powers, and on the limits of authority even in emergencies. In general, this literature is heavily legalistic, warmly polemical, and probably only tangentially useful for the purposes of teaching and research, except to illuminate the tensions of a time and place.

On the other hand, some authors have paid more than lip service to the constitutionalism they frequently claim as their primary concern and have held to a standard of constitutionalism that Thomas Jefferson described in his first inaugural address in 1801: "the text of civil instruction—the touchstone by which to try the services of those we trust."* The following suggestions for further reading attempt to reach toward this high standard, as well as to direct teachers and students toward unideological, balanced analyses.

Because space limitations kept many deserving titles from this compilation, one should consult appropriate portions of the *Harvard Guide to American History,* ed. Frank Freidel, 2 vols., rev. ed. (Cambridge, Mass., 1974); *A Comprehensive Bibliography of American Constitutional and Legal History,* ed. Kermit L. Hall, 5 vols. (Millwood, N.Y., 1984); William E. Nelson and John P. Reid, *The Literature of American Legal History* (New York, 1985); and the bibliography in Alfred H. Kelly, Winfred Harbison, and Herman Belz, *The American Constitution,* 6th ed. (New York, 1983), 768-842, esp. 833-35. Other guides to special concerns include the very helpful compilation by John Slonaker, "The U.S. Army and Domestic Disturbances" (typescript, U.S. Army Military History Research Collection, Carlisle Barracks, Pa., 1970), and bibliographies on "War and Emergency Legislation" (Air University Library, Maxwell Air Force Base, Alabama, n.d.). In addition, there are troves of unpublished research in the American Bar Association's War Powers Study Papers, Columbia University Rare Book and Manuscript Library. Harold Relyea's *A Brief History of Emergency Powers in the United States: A Working Paper. Prepared for the [Senate] Special Committee on National Emergencies and Delegated Emergency Powers,*

**Messages and Papers of the Presidents, 1789-1897,* ed. James D. Richardson (New York, 1901), 324. Michael Kammen's "Problem of Constitutionalism in American Culture" (Bicentennial Lecture, University of Dallas, 24 April 1985), 1, a significant statement, accepts "civic" instead of "civil" in Jefferson's sentence.

93d Cong., 2d sess. (Washington, 1974), is the most exhaustive guide to episodes involving the uses of war and emergency powers to 1974.

War and emergency powers are examined carefully and imaginatively in Carl J. Friedrich, *Constitutional Reason of State: The Survival of the Constitutional Order* (Providence, R.I., 1957), and Clinton L. Rossiter, *Constitutional Dictatorship: Crisis Government in Modern Democracies* (Princeton, 1948). The benefits of comparative explorations are evident in Allan Dershowitz, "Preventive Detention of Citizens During a National Emergency—A Comparison Between Israel and the United States," *Israel Yearbook of Human Rights,* I (1971): 295; Cecil T. Carr, "Crisis Legislation in Britain," *Columbia Law Review,* 40 (1940): 1309; Olga Mladenovic, ed., *The Yugoslav Concept of General People's Defense,* trans. Kordija Kveder et al. (Belgrade, 1970); and Stanford Research Institute, *A Study of the Emergency Regulations of Malaya, 1948-1960* (Palo Alto, Ca., 1967). Broader inquiries include Edward Keynes, *Undeclared War* (University Park, Pa., 1982); Fritz Grob, *The Relativity of War and Peace: A Study of Law, History, and Politics* (New Haven, 1949); and Reginald C. Stuart, *War and American Thought: From the Revolution to the Monroe Doctrine* (Kent, Oh., 1982).

Of the unending efforts to discover the "intent" of the Constitution's Framers concerning war and emergency powers, the most useful include Charles A. Lofgren, "War-Making Under the Constitution: The Original Understanding," *Yale Law Journal,* 81 (1972): 672; W. Taylor Reveley III, *War Powers of the President and Congress: Who Holds the Arrows and Olive Branch?* (Charlottesville, Va., 1981); Abraham D. Sofaer, *War, Foreign Affairs, and Constitutional Power: The Origins* (Cambridge, Mass., 1976); Francis L. Coolidge and Joel D. Sharrow, "The War-Making Powers: The Intentions of the Framers in the Light of Parliamentary History," *Boston University Law Review,* 50 (1970): 1; Bernard Donahoe and Marshall Smelser, "The Congressional Power to Raise Armies: The Constitutional & Ratifying Conventions, 1787-1788," *Review of Politics,* 33 (1971): 202; and Merlo J. Pusey, *The Way We Go To War* (Boston, 1969). All concur that leadership in these matters, though bent toward Congress, has oscillated between the White House and Capitol Hill during the past two centuries without overstraining the designs, perceptions, and aspirations of 1787.

This preponderance favoring congressional initiatives, however, has not lessened the president-centeredness of chroniclers and historians from Parson Weems's and George Bancroft's times to ours. Arthur M. Schlesinger, jr., *The Imperial Presidency* (Boston, 1973), and *The Ultimate Decision: The President as Commander in Chief,* ed. Ernest R. May (New York, 1960), are deservedly popular surveys of the theme and provide excellent teaching and study materials. Variant views on executive powers can be found in G. Malcolm Smith and Cornelius P. Crotter, *Powers of the President During Crisis* (New York, 1960); Ann V. Thomas, *War-Making Powers of the President* (Dallas, 1982); *The Tethered Presidency: Congressional Restraints on Executive Power,* ed. Thomas M. Franck (New York, 1981); and in older but still useful expressions, Clarence E. Berdahl, *War Powers of the Executive in the United States* (Urbana, Il., 1921), and Bennet M. Rich, *The Presidents and Civil Disorder* (Washington, 1941).

Well-balanced efforts to trace concurrent relationships in the war powers between president and Congress include Thomas M. Franck and Edward Weisband, *Foreign Policy by Congress* (New York, 1979); Louis Henkin, *Foreign Affairs and the Constitution* (Mineola, N.Y., 1972); Don Wallace, Jr., "The War-Making Power: A Constitutional Flaw?" *Cornell Law Review,* 57 (1972): 719; and William B. Spong, Jr., "Can Balance Be Restored in the Constitutional War Powers of the President and Congress?" *University of Richmond Law Review,* 6 (1971): 1.

It becomes unhappily obvious that Americans have studied the presidency and the judiciary far more frequently, intensively, and systematically than Congress. Indeed, it may be that the United States is the only major Western nation that possesses no full-scale scholarly history of its national legislature, and this in our Bicentennial season! Hope exists for improvement in this deplorable situation. A decade ago the Senate created a historian's office, and last year the House of Representatives followed suit. These commendable operations are likely to become centers of congressional scholarship in themselves and sources of encouragement to historians and other scholars nationwide and abroad with interests in Capitol Hill operations.

While we wait for more systematically illuminating histories of Congress with respect to war and emergency powers, we can occupy ourselves usefully and almost endlessly with inquiries about the judiciary's proper role in deciding such political questions. Of the inquiries that Vietnam evoked, John Norton Moore's "Justiciability of Challenges to the Use of Military Forces Abroad," *Virginia Journal of International Law,* 10 (1969): 85, and Michael E. Tigar, "Judicial Power, the 'Political Question Doctrine,' and Foreign Relations," *UCLA Law Review,* 17 (1970): 1135, both raise the basic questions that transcend the Vietnam context in commendably nontechnical terms.

The virtually inexhaustible and seemingly insuppressible phenomenon of political murder that is so spectacular in our time receives careful attention in Franklin L. Ford, *Political Murder: From Tyrannicide to Terrorism* (Cambridge, Mass., 1985).

DCP3/86 1.2M